POLITICS AND ETHICS

POLITICS AND ETHICS

Patterns in Partnership

by
Francis X. Winters, S.J.

PAULIST PRESS
New York / Paramus / Toronto

Library of Congress
Catalog Card Number: 74-27732

ISBN: 0-8091-1862-9

COVER DESIGN: Emil Antonucci

Published by Paulist Press
Editorial Office: 1865 Broadway, N.Y., N.Y. 10023
Business Office: 400 Sette Drive, Paramus, N.J. 07652

Printed and bound in the
United States of America

172
W78

Contents

Paulist/Newman Press

21 Jan 76   1 ©

54511

*To
my mother and father*

Editor's Introduction

Francis X. Winters, a professor of Christian Ethics at Georgetown, offers in this book a moral argument that combines original model-building with practical application to specific problems in political ethics.

"Political morality," writes Fr. Winters, "is held to consist in the effort to universalize (apply to all others) the rights that one demands for oneself." Hence, political morality speaks to Tennyson's question: "Ah, when will all men's good be each man's rule, and universal peace lie like a shaft of light across the land?" And in discussing political morality, this book sends its own shaft of light on some of the shadows and ambiguities of national decision-making in America.

The argument developed in these pages could inspire some sober reflection in the United States as this nation celebrates its Bicentennial. According to Fr. Winters, no American foreign policy decision should be inconsistent with the philosophy of power that resides in the Constitution of the United States. "If the United States claims self-determination as its own right (and as the right of each of its citizens), it is obliged for the sake of consistency to grant this same right of self-determination to all other nations which do not disqualify themselves as partners in the international political system by unjust or expansionist policies." As we celebrate 200 years of self-determination, we can find in the very principle we praise an ethical norm for measuring our military involvement in foreign lands, our foreign investment, foreign trade and foreign aid, to mention just a few international issues of great ethical import.

The theory of partnership ("a relationship of mutual dependence and reciprocal influence"), which is developed in the first half of this book, is presented by the author as a new base for moral decision-making. He then applies this theory to Watergate, Vietnam and the problem of limited warfare, and thus gives the reader a new perspective on familiar problems. That the "new" perspective happens to be ethical is itself an indication of our long-standing, unmet need for ethical reflection on great national problems. This book is a welcome contribution toward meeting that need.

The suggestion that greater stress should be placed on social process rather than cognitive principles in moral decision-making will, as the author admits, "remain the subject of debate for decades to come." But one can only admire the skill of this practicing ethician and welcome the moral light he sheds on complex political problems. By arguing that the partnership paradigm, if accepted by decision-makers as morally normative, would have shortened our involvement in Vietnam, prevented Watergate, and, by prompting us to offer conditional surrender to Germany and Japan, precluded the use of the atomic bomb in 1945, Fr. Winters demonstrates some of the uses of this kind of ethical theory. But before it can be used, it has to be known and discussed. *Politics and Ethics* is presented with the hope that it will add to our knowledge and stimulate our interest in the theory and practice of political ethics.

William J. Byron, S.J.
Loyola University, New Orleans

Foreword

This book represents the reflections of a Roman Catholic moralist who has been striving personally and professionally for the last twenty years to reconcile the divergent moral traditions he has encountered in religious America. Educated and nurtured in a Roman Catholic culture which was continental in its style, I discovered the treasures of the American Protestant moral tradition ten years ago. Since that time these two styles of moral thought, apparently quite alien to one another, have been vying for my intellectual allegiance. More recently, the fundamental complementarity of the two traditions has become more apparent to me, suggesting the possibility of outlining a more comprehensive approach to Christian ethics. In the belief that many of my fellow Catholics have experienced a similar wavering between these moral theories, I have attempted to set out here an interpretation of the moral life that incorporates some insights of each of these traditions under a new rubric: that of partnership, a morality based on the maintenance of relationships of mutual dependence and reciprocal influence.

The key element in the notion of partnership is the perception that moral wisdom is more liable to be found in one's fellow human beings than in moral principles. Both Roman Catholics, with their characteristic moral theory of the natural law, and contemporary Protestant moralists, such as H. Richard Niebuhr, who favor a "contextualist" approach to ethics, have highlighted the social resources for achieving ethical insight. In the Roman Catholic tradition, for example, natural law theory reserved a privileged place for the authority of "the wise" who could properly interpret the precise application of moral principles to specific circumstances. While St. Thomas himself, following the Platonic tradition, seems to have reserved the privilege of moral interpretation to a few exceptionally well-informed persons who combined moral rectitude and technical expertise (*Summa Theologica*, I-II, q. 100), the role of authority in Roman Catholicism was gradually diffused to all professional moralists, whose internal consensus constituted the determination of moral values. In the course of this "bureaucratization" of wisdom, the genuine utility of authority in moral discernment was undoubtedly obscured, as a casual perusal of any moral textbook will reveal. Yet the basic insight that moral principles are not themselves adequate to provide moral guidance without the assistance of some authoritative interpretation is a perennially valid one. Classical natural law theory included the influence of a hierarchical authority as a constitutive element in the formation of Christian conscience.

American Protestantism likewise resisted the effort to propagate self-applying moral principles. Authors such as H. Richard Niebuhr, Paul Lehmann, and Gibson Winter underlined the necessity for authoritative interpretation of moral principles. Predictably, however, these authors, influenced by the Reformation's skepticism toward hierarchical authority in religious matters, located this authority in the horizontal and reciprocal influence of members of society (and of the Church, in particular) on one another. Undoubtedly the American political preference for horizontal structures of authority influenced this perception of the role of religious and moral authority as well.

Despite this profound difference of political philosophy, however, which accounts for the divergent roles assigned to moral authorities (for Catholics, a hierarchical function, and, for Protestants, a more democratic role), the two traditions agree on the indispensability of consultation prior to decision-making. Neither tradition accepts the solitary conscience as the sole arbiter of morals, for such solipsism would neglect the vast resources of experience and insight available in the community. "Contextualism" is the usual Protestant designation of ethical theories which rely on collaboration in the process of discernment, while Catholics (since Vatican II) make a similar affirmation of the social nature of conscience when they speak of "collegiality." There are, of course, confessionally determined differences of accent between "collegiality," which connotes ceremonial gatherings of ecclesiastical hierarchy, and "contextualism," which suggests rather the influence of everyday social interaction on an individual's moral choices. Yet the area of agreement between the traditions is ample: it lies in the acceptance of authority, or the validity of social influence, for one's own moral decision. It is to underline this ecumenically shared perception of the social resources of an individual's moral life that I have focused these reflections on the image of partnership, by which I mean something approximating the spirit of contextualism or collegiality.

The opening essay, which emphasizes the potential value of social processes for moral decision-making, suggests the need to reconceptualize the function of moral principles. It suggests, in effect, that (1) the commitment to explore the moral resources of social process is itself a principle, and perhaps the fundamental principle of the moral life; (2) the conscientious commitment to social interaction implies the inevitability of certain other principles, such as the necessity for truthful communication among social partners; (3) social processes themselves are malleable and finite and therefore always capable of reform and extension to embrace previously excluded individuals; social process is itself dependent on the observance of certain moral principles if it is to remain an adequate moral guide. Since this is an essay in Christian ethics, it concludes with reflections on some of the specifically Christian characteristics of social process.

Moral theory, even a theory based on partnership, is necessarily abstruse. It is, however, one of the traditional virtues of Catholic moral theory to cling close to specific cases. In continuity with this tradition, the essay on partnership is followed by another which attempts to apply the theory to three contemporary problems in political ethics: "Watergate"; the moral validity of national interest as a criterion of foreign policy; and the adequacy of the just war theory in a nuclear age. It is hoped that the implications of the more theoretical essay will be clarified in the essay on political ethics.

There is, unfortunately, no discussion included of the implications of partnership for private or inter-personal ethics. The omission is unfortunate, since personal relations, including their sexual dimension, constitute the most obvious application of a moral theory of partnership. They constitute as well one of the most confused areas of moral discussion. The omission is nevertheless deliberate, for the author's professional competence does not qualify him to explore these problems in writing.

Finally, a note on format. Since these essays are not technical, I have spared the reader (and the author?) the burden of scholarly apparatus. At the conclusion of each section of the initial essay, however, I have listed the authors whose works have guided my own thinking, and, in some cases, I have offered some brief reflections on their works.

In closing I would like to express my gratitude to the Reverend William J. Byron, S.J., who invited me to join in this series of publications, and to my colleagues at Georgetown who assisted in preparation of the manuscript.

> Francis X. Winters, S.J.
> School of Foreign Service
> Georgetown University

Cove Cottage
Centreville, Maryland
May 1074

I
Ethics

1. Partnership

Modern man, in his effort to live morally, has no need of absolute principles. Such principles are illusory guides to action which often lead to arbitrary and inhuman choices. In place of such principles, a conscientious person can rely on the dynamics of social processes to lead him to a correct decision. By committing himself to the process of partnership with others, a person can jointly discern the fitting action in any situation. There is no possibility or need of principles. Process is the principle.

This contemporary manifesto could be subscribed to by a wide variety of contemporary thinkers and probably expresses the moral sentiments of a majority of educated Americans under 30 years of age. Is this formula adequate for leading a moral life in contemporary America? That is, is it true?

The essay which follows will argue that the manifesto is *very nearly* true. It is neither the whole truth, nor merely a "half-truth." Rather it comes close to expressing the whole truth about morality and it can be understood to imply the rest of the truth. It is, in short, an adequate summary of morality *if understood correctly*. In the present chapter I would like to reflect on the truth of the statement, its essential accuracy. In the following chapter, our considerations will turn to those implications of its essential truth which must be made explicit if the manifesto is not to be misleading. The first chapter then will deal with the essential relationship between social process (partnership) and ethics. Subsequently (chapter 2), it will become evident that partnership itself implies adherence to certain constant patterns of human behavior, such as truthfulness, which can legitimately be understood as moral principles. Without adherence to some such principles, the social process itself will perish. Then, in the final chapter, an effort will be made to establish the religious context in which a believer makes his moral decisions.

Partnership

There is more strength and creativity in certain relationships among individuals than in the individuals alone. The ethics of partnership reflects on this fact and considers the types and contexts of relationships which are liable to release the energy hidden in individuals. Most simply, such an ethics claims that human beings are most creative and contented when they share in a relationship of reciprocal influence and mutual dependence. On the basis of this realization, most individual choices can be called "good" or "bad" insofar as they promote or inhibit such mutual influence and interdependence.

It may be helpful in trying to understand these claims to reflect on the single notable exception to this rule. That exception is contemplation. Probably alone among all significant and satisfying human activities, contemplation, which may after all be the highest human achievement, can be attained by an individual in solitude. Indeed, a variety of philosophies and religions maintain that solitude is the indispensable prerequisite to contemplation. Even those who aspire to be "contemplatives in action" insist on an inner detachment from society, and some religions associate the gift of contemplation with celibacy—a life-style of solitude. Plotinus' definition of the contemplative state, "the flight of the alone to the Alone," represents, therefore, an ancient and accurate tradition of philosophical or religious discovery.

With this notable exception, however, there may be no deeply enriching experience which can be attained apart from others. Love leaps to the mind as mankind's richest treasure. What is best in life—affection, admiration and association—can neither be attained in private nor even be controlled by a single individual. Love is a mutual attainment, or simply an illusion. Lovers depend on one another for the meager and fragile meaning they hope to find in life. The mysterious journey of love cannot be taken alone.

In H. Richard Niebuhr's study entitled *The Purpose of the Church and Its Ministry*, there is a passage on love which expresses the experience of partnership eloquently.

By love we mean at least these attitudes and actions: rejoicing in the presence of the beloved, gratitude, reverence and loyalty toward him. Love is rejoicing over the existence of the beloved one; it is the desire that he be rather than not be; it is longing for his presence when he is absent; it is happiness in the thought of him; it is profound satisfaction over everything that makes him great and glorious. Love is gratitude: it is thankfulness for the existence of the beloved; it is the happy acceptance of everything that he gives without the jealous feeling that the self ought to be able to do as much; it is a gratitude that does not seek equality; it is wonder over the other's gift of himself in companionship. Love is reverence: it keeps its distance even as it draws near; it does not seek to absorb the other in the self or want to be absorbed by it; it rejoices in the otherness of the other; it desires the beloved to be what he is and does not seek to refashion him into a replica of the self or to make him a means to the self's advancement. As reverence love is and seeks knowledge of the other, not by way of curiosity nor for the sake of gaining power but in rejoicing and in wonder. In all such love there is an element of that "holy fear" which is not a form of flight but rather deep respect for the otherness of the beloved and the profound unwillingness to violate his integrity. Love is loyalty; it is the willingness to let the self be destroyed rather than that the other cease to be; it is the commitment of the self by self-binding will to make the other great. It is loyalty, too, to the other's cause—to his loyalty.

Affection is the most obvious example of the almost universal nexus between partnership—a relationship of mutual dependence and reciprocal influence —and human happiness. But many other spheres of activity would serve almost as well to illustrate the point that man was not made to live alone. Indeed, the emergence of a new sense of the importance of partnership may be one of the central insights which ties together a variety of contemporary social movements in religion, education and politics.

For American Catholics, for example, collegiality (along with the reform of the liturgy) was the central discovery of the Second Vatican Council. Schooled in the doctrine of papal infallibility, several generations of clergy and laity alike were confronted by the Council with a profound revolution in organizational structure and philosophical outlook. They were told that they themselves had a contribution to make to the ongoing process of church governance. They had, in short, a voice: a right and a duty to contribute to the decision-making processes in the church, from the level of the parish right up to the Papacy. Collegiality is nothing more than a theological term for political partnership: cooperation in church governance. The word implies the desirability, even the indispensability, of joint deliberation and decision-making among appointed leaders and the people. Collegiality is a revolution in church structure based on the growing awareness of the dignity of the individual as a sharer in the church's task of self-determination. In the post-Vatican II church, neither the leaders alone nor the faithful alone but the two together are the source of wisdom on the meaning and role of religious life.

Similarly, educational reform in the United States is being shaped by a vision of co-responsibility for the tasks of scholarship and instruction. Both on the level of school governance and within the classroom itself there is a current tendency to accept the influence of various points of view, including those of the students themselves. An influential book like Paulo Freire's *Pedagogy of the Oppressed* is nothing more than an elaboration of the insight that teachers and students can discover their respective identities only if they learn first to see themselves as co-investigators, as teacher-students and student-teachers. A creative classroom is one in which the learning task is seen either as a joint effort to answer pressing human questions, or at least as a propaedeutic to such shared investigation.

America's present constitutional crisis, deepened and perhaps ultimately to be alleviated by the Watergate scandal, reveals an analogous struggle to reinstitutionalize a process of joint decision-making between the

legislative and executive branches of the government.
Prodded by the gradual mis-appropriation of power to
the White House, the American people seem on the
verge of reasserting the constitutional system of checks
and balances. In government, as well as in religion and
education, shared responsibility is widely accepted as
the solution to the contemporary crisis.

There is emerging a growing appreciation of partnership in public as well as in private life. What, then,
is the nature of such sharing? What are its qualities and
dynamics? A variety of contemporary authors have suggested some characteristics of partnership, including:
complementarity, mutuality, reciprocity, symmetry,
communication, and creative conflict. All of these attempts at description echo the fundamental qualities of
partnership, namely, mutual dependence and reciprocal
influence.

Inspiring all these attempts by various contemporary authors to describe the dynamics of a creative
relationship is a common conviction that two attitudes
are required on the part of individuals if they are to
become partners. The first pre-requisite is *self-respect*.
Viewed negatively, self-respect implies that the individual is entering the relationship not out of any sense of
inadequacy or overwhelming need, but rather out of the
conviction that the human task is so constructed that it
can be accomplished only in concert. More positively,
this quality arises from a feeling of self-acceptance,
self-reliance, even self-love. Only one who trusts himself is finally able to trust another. The starting point of
partnership then is a healthy attitude of self-sufficiency.

On the basis of such self-acceptance, the individual
can easily develop the second characteristic which con-

tributes to personal relationships: *trust in others*. Probably the clearest historical example of this quality was the pedagogical philosophy of Socrates, who never taught others but merely inquired of them, in order to bring out the understanding of reality hidden within them. "Dialogue" was a way of life for Socrates because he considered dialogue to be the basic structure of social reality. Given a context of confidence, he believed, any individual could discover the truth within himself. When we recall this simple key to Socratic thought, Paulo Freire's "new pedagogy" seems not so revolutionary after all. Essentially, Socrates had said it all before.

Each generation has its own Socrates, however, and our own Socrates was Gandhi. With an essentially identical approach to truth, the Mahatma articulated an approach to politics which consisted in staging confrontations which would require the opponent to face the truth in himself. From such dialogue or confrontations would emerge the truth for the situation. Although Gandhi is best known for his political achievements and almost equally identified with a philosophy of non-violence, it is important to realize that for Gandhi himself the basic issue was *truth*. What actions of his own or of his followers would reveal the truth of the situation? The answer was always: those actions which would engage the adversary in continuing confrontation without destroying him. For this reason, Gandhi felt required to advocate non-violence, since destroying an opponent, who possessed his own segment of the truth, would preclude the possibility of discovering that truth. At the heart of *Ahimsa* (non-violence) is the search for truth through dialogue. Prior to non-

violence in the Gandhian philosophy, then, is respect
for others as bearers of the truth. Here once more we
see the dialectic of self-respect and respect for the
partner. Without either conviction, an individual cannot
become a partner.

Two-way communication is the pattern of partnership. Such reciprocity springs from the assurance
that neither I nor my partner has the whole truth but
that together we may discover it. While talking about
such two-way communication may be easy enough, it is
necessary to talk about it precisely because it so rarely
happens. Most conversations as well as most social situations are marred by exaggerated self-assurance or
profound diffidence. Somewhere between these two
closed stances lies the creative attitude, demonstrated
by Socrates and Gandhi, of mutual dependence and reciprocal influence.

Genuine communication arises only from two independent centers of personal initiative and response.
For this reason communication builds upon self-respect
and trust in others. For the same reason communication is inextricably associated with conflict. In
addition to the required qualities of self-esteem and
trust, then, partnership supposes another characteristic
in the individual: a *positive evaluation of conflict.* Here,
the ethics of partnership runs into a cultural barrier: the
widespread conviction that harmony or consensus is the
ideal pattern for human relationships. Arising from this
preference for peace (the absence of *open* disagreement)
is the reluctance to express differences of opinion and
to seek the resolution of conflict through argument and
mutual adjustment. Without an appreciation for the
creative potential of conflict, relationships often sink to

the level of non-controversial communication, which is almost surely conversation about the inconsequential. It is probably fair to say that a relationship without open conflict is superficial and doomed to transiency.

Creative conflict, then, is another characteristic of productive partnership. Obviously, not all conflict is creative. Conflict can be mere wrangling. In order to make conflict creative, the parties to the dispute must be committed to working through the conflict and adjusting their prior claims in the light of the argument. Accommodation is not possible if either party, or both, is so committed to one possible outcome that he is unwilling to consider the alternative.

This observation about the flexibility required of partners in a lasting relationship may seem rather banal. But it is precisely here that the ethics of partnership takes issue with many previous ethical models, including the one most familiar to Catholics, that of the natural law. On this point, the moral model being proposed here is closer to the Gandhian approach to life, which has only one immutable value, namely, the *single-minded search for the truth*. A corollary of this singleness of purpose is the second principle of Gandhi, that the truth-seeker (as Gandhi always described himself) must be *indifferent to all other values*. Otherwise, the partners, or counterplayers, will not be able to confront one another at the most profound level, and so discover the truth. Commitment to the process of partnership implies a questioning of all other commitments, even of all other moral principles. The Gandhian ethic is revolutionary, for it demands that partners can confront one another absolutely free of prejudgment about the outcome of their encounter. Even the possibility of discontinuing the relationship itself must be left open to discussion. Perhaps separation is the truth for them. Commitment to the process of partnership thus displaces all other values, including the value of encountering this particular partner.

Partnership, then, is the phenomenon of purposeful and sustained sharing between two individuals who subordinate their other preferences to this union in the conviction that only through such personal communication can they discover the meaning of life. In order to maintain such a relationship, the partners must be self-reliant individuals capable of freely becoming dependent on one another and trusting enough to initiate spontaneously and to respond creatively. From such a partnership each individual derives the satisfaction of continual discovery and significant achievement, and through the relationship their personal complementarity is heightened and enriched.

We have observed that partnership is most often associated with affective intimacy. Yet reflection on the phenomenon reveals a genuine analogy between love and friendship and a host of other relationships, such as the bond that unites teachers with students, citizens with leaders, laymen with the hierarchy. In all these social situations it is possible to experience the mutual dependence, the reciprocal influence, the give-and-take which constitutes communication. Indeed, partnership is a central phenomenon of life, one of its most satisfying experiences.

But is it more? Is partnership the most basic structure of existence? Does it constitute a paradigm of life itself? Is it possible to *evaluate* virtually all experiences on the basis of mutuality, complementarity, communication? If so, the analysis of partnership suggests an ethics of partnership, a new theory of the moral life. We will test this hypothesis in the following section.

Partnership: A Moral Paradigm

By speaking of ethical choice, the preeminent realm of spontaneity or freedom, with images which suggest determinism, such as "pattern" or "paradigm," one seems almost to be indulging in paradox for its own sake. On reflection, however, it becomes clear that the paradox exists in the human situation itself, which is a mysterious blend of freedom and form. Further meditation on the patterns that can be traced in human spontaneity thus leads us to a more profound understanding of the human condition. Because there are patterns evident in the human phenomenon of freedom, it is possible to understand morality with the help of paradigms, such as that of partnership.

Paradigm is usually understood as a pattern of activity—linguistic or sheerly intellectual—which is subject to certain fixed laws and which occurs largely without premeditation or conscious selection. Paradigms are expressions or explanations of routine or repetitive actions. Morality, on the other hand, is normally associated with precisely the opposite sort of activity, that which is consciously selected, unpredictable, even inexplicable by general statements. Morality will be described in the following chapter precisely as resistance to expected behavior, as non-conformity. How then is it possible to explain the phenomenon of morality by this paradoxical juncture of "moral" and "paradigm"?

"Paradigm" has returned to common usage recently through the broadly influential work of Thomas S. Kuhn, *The Structure of Scientific Revolutions*. Kuhn uses this expression to signify an intellectual hypothesis which is commonly shared in a culture or in a sub-culture, such as the scientific community. He suggests that scientific epochs are marked by the general acceptance of a fundamental perspective on the way certain phenomena occur, for example, the relative motion of celestial bodies. During the height of a certain scientific era, most observed phenomena can be readily explained by a certain paradigm, or scientific hypothesis, such as Ptolemaic astronomy. Gradually, however, an increasing number of anomalous observations are made, which cannot easily be reconciled with the conventional model of astronomy. The accumulation of such observations which are inexplicable in terms of the prevalent theory creates a crisis in the scientific community, which experiences the need to find a new hypothesis to account for the facts. When such a new theory appears, it meets widespread resistance from conventional thinkers, but finally prevails because of its ability to interpret reality more adequately than the previous model. Thus a new paradigm is born, as happened in the case of the Copernican revolution.

In this sense, moral theory has been going through a critical period at least since the end of World War II, but more likely since the turn of the century (when Ernst Troeltsch announced at the end of his survey of Christian ethics that "new thoughts will have to be thought.") The matched atrocities of the Axis powers and the Allies during the forties, culminating in the obliteration- and atom-bombing that brought the war to a close, revealed the inadequacy of the dominant moral models to restrain violence and provide security for the species. There was a widely felt need to get back to the ethical drawing board.

Early efforts to reestablish a moral consensus fluctuated between a renaissance of natural law thinking, which aspired to establish a supra-legal code whereby citizens could sit in judgment on governmental actions, and the elaboration of situation ethics, a non-theory which tried to turn exceptions into the rule. Neither of these formulations has won wide acceptance, for reasons which are suggested in the following chapter. At any rate, the ethical crisis is still a source of widespread anxiety and the search for an acceptable moral paradigm goes on.

While the scientific sense of paradigm is the most frequently used one, we might find as much insight into the function of paradigms by recalling the grammatical or linguistic use of the word. In grammar, paradigms consist in sequential listings of the variable parts of word forms, such as the declension of nouns and the conjugation of verbs. These paradigms illustrate the proper forms for various categories of words when they have a specified function. For example, each of the five classes of Latin nouns has a fixed ending when used as subject or object of a verb. There are exceptions to these rules, which do not themselves occur frequently enough to merit separate categorization or paradigms. These exceptions are simply memorized by students of the language, while all "regular" nouns can be correctly used simply by applying the paradigmatic endings to whatever word-stem falls into a specific category (declension). Paradigms, in other words, are models of correct usage for various types of words. They represent the linguistic conventions of a culture.

From this description of a linguistic paradigm arises the paradox of "moral paradigms," for morality always signifies a critical review of conventional behavior. "Morality" seems to exclude the predetermination implied in "paradigms." It was this seeming antinomy between morality and the patterned activity implied in the use of paradigms, perhaps, that gave rise to the theory of situationism. "Theorists" of the new morality were trying to design a moral language without rules, purely spontaneous selection of actions. It is no wonder that their unfinished tower stands as a reminder of the continuing crisis in ethical thought, for the presupposition of the system, namely, that some human activities can transcend patterns, turned out to be false. Even freedom has its own pattern, which post-situationists must now go on to discover. It is, of course, the thesis of this essay that partnership is a helpful paradigm of freedom.

In suggesting that freedom operates according to certain structures or paradigms, it is well to recall that many native speakers of a language attain eloquence without any awareness of the grammatical patterns present in their language. Speech, even eloquence, is no more dependent on grammatical knowledge than goodness is on ethical analysis. But anyone who aspires to share with another his linguistic abilities will soon fall back on the use of paradigms. Recognition and communication of patterns is essential to the teaching process, in linguistics as well as in morality. Perhaps, then, the expression "moral paradigm" is acceptable after all, notwithstanding the paradox it implies.

What is meant by a moral paradigm here is an image of human activity verified in so wide a variety of free choices that it helps the moral agent to understand the patterns present in his own activity and assists him in sharing this understanding with others. By speaking of partnership as a moral paradigm, we mean that partnership—the maintenance of relationships in which two persons depend on one another and influence one another—is a pattern present in a vast majority of free and therefore significant human activities. Furthermore this image of partnership can be helpful in improving the quality of one's own actions and in introducing others to a richer experience in life. "Partnership" is therefore both descriptive and prescriptive: a paradigm of morality.

The paradox implied in speaking of partnership as a moral paradigm is, however, even more subtle and more substantial than we have implied above. That paradox is revealed whenever one begins to communicate to others the realization that there are patterns of activity which are not merely descriptive of the past and present but prescriptive as well and that an image such as partnership *should* serve to guide one's choices and direct one's activities. The almost invariable initial response to such talk about prescriptive ethics is cynicism, a deep and almost unconscious belief that the only real pattern in human activity is unfreedom, the determination of individual choices by overwhelming forces of self-interest and the search for survival. This reaction is especially disturbing when it comes, almost unbidden, from young adults, who often seem to have accepted a primitive fatalism even before they have tested the limits of freedom for themselves. The typical reaction to discourse about morality in politics, for example, is something like: "Politics has always been simply a question of power. It will always be that way. Don't fool yourself by asking about alternatives. Human beings always act out of self-interest. Talking about political ethics is sheer hypocrisy." There is in our culture, or perhaps in human nature itself, a deep preference for the patterns of the past over the possibilities of the future. Fate still seems to be the god who is worshipped in the silence of the heart. The instinct for freedom, for overturning the past by initiating a new future, is fragile indeed. Almost universally, people prefer paradigms to morality. We are, then, dealing with a central paradox of life when we speak of moral paradigms. Indeed, most people are too cynical to believe that such a paradox exists, because they believe in fate more than they believe in freedom. Perhaps the crucial difference between the moral man or woman and the amoral one lies precisely here in their respective convictions about whether freedom is a possibility or only an illusion.

Within this context of almost universal cynicism, it becomes apparent that moral discourse is of crucial importance to civilization, for it is through speaking about morality that one person communicates to another, or one generation shares with its successors, the fragile vision of freedom. Speaking about morality is itself an act of freedom and therefore a risk, for one never knows whether one is speaking to the deaf. Moral discourse is an effort to establish partnership among those who believe that the future is as real as the past, that there may be a way out of the present crisis. Moral discourse attempts to establish a partnership of resistance to pessimism.

It is to this deep and almost unconquerable fatalism that the Bible in its entirety is addressed. From the opening scene of *Genesis* onward, the stories in our sacred books confront us with the challenge to choose the future, a future which we cannot see. The biblical challenge is the challenge to be free of the past by accepting the future. For example, the temptation of Adam and Eve to eat fruit from the tree of the knowledge of good and evil depicts the perennial human predicament: to be required to make choices about a future which is shrouded in darkness. When prohibited by God from eating this fruit, Adam and Eve were required to make crucial choices for their own future and for their descendants without any sure knowledge of how these choices would turn out. God's prerogative of omniscience was denied them and yet they were commanded to emulate God's freedom—his ability to choose between alternative courses of action. Thus they were placed squarely in the predicament which all of us face, of risking our present security by reaching for a better future. To refuse that risk, as the first couple did by insisting on prior knowledge of the future, is to commit the primeval and perennial sin of refusing to enter into the human condition of blind choice. The punishment for that sin (symbolized by expulsion from the garden) is the ultimate imprisonment, confinement to the past. Liberation from that curse comes through choosing the future without benefit of foreknowledge. Only through risk can mankind escape imprisonment.

The paradox implied in the notion of a "moral paradigm" is resolved only by grace, as we will see below (chapter 3), when we discuss the relation between morality and mystery. At present it must suffice to say that the almost inevitably cynical response to the challenge of morality is not simply a current cultural phenomenon. It is the human condition of sin and therefore the locus of redemption. To overcome the human predisposition to cling to the past is to be saved.

Rudolph Bultmann, a distinguished German exegete who likewise was capable of interpreting the scriptures in a fashion intelligible to contemporary culture, realized that the philosophy of Heidegger was an eloquent statement of the concept of salvation through self-determination. Using (faithfully or not, I am unable to determine) Heidegger's interpretation of human existence, Bultmann described the moral life as: "openness to the future," "the capacity to strive for a goal," or "will." For him, man is the being whose fate it is to live under the necessity of decision. Man, to become man, must decide. While Bultmann's understanding of salvation is not comprehensive, as we will argue in a subsequent chapter, it is utterly true to the scriptures as far as it goes. Man's fate is to escape from fate by choosing his own future, which always remains hidden to him. Without risk there is no escape from the human predicament.

How then can one choose? What are the grounds that allow one to choose one course rather than another? Is ethics anything more than another version of random selection? In choosing the mysterious future, to what can one look for guidance? If the theme of this essay is correct, this final question should be rephrased in this way: To *whom* can one look for guidance? Here I think we can glimpse finally the full meaning of our paradoxical title: "partnership as a moral paradigm." The answer proposed here to the puzzle of morality is this: that only by choosing a hidden future can one escape the prison of the past, and only by joining in partnership with another person can one choose the future wisely. Perhaps this is why we read, in the same book of *Genesis*, that it is not good for man to be alone. The meaning of our title, then, is *the imperative of part-*

nership: each of us must choose to choose together with someone and, further, we must choose together with whom we will choose.

We will return to this theme of shared discernment in the following chapter, in a treatment of "collegial wisdom." For the time being it may suffice to offer a simple answer to the question raised at the outset of this chapter: Is the modern manifesto, which opened this essay, a true vision of the moral life? Can social process replace moral principle? Is partnership a paradigm, or image, of morality which can replace earlier models, such as those of deontology and teleology? Have we a new paradigm of morality in the notion of partnership?

Only time and wide acceptance will tell whether partnership is in fact the new paradigm so widely sought. If, however, partnership were accepted as an interpretive symbol of the moral life, the adoption of this new paradigm would imply that there is a structure of freedom which does not operate automatically. Freedom must be exploited by conscious choice, specifically by the effort to maintain relationships of mutual dependence and reciprocal influence in all levels of society from intimate friendship to international relations.

The choice of partnership as a paradigm, however, need not mean the rejection of moral principles. For this reason, it is impossible simply to endorse the opening manifesto. There are many forms of partnership which depend on the proper employment of moral principles to maintain interdependence and reciprocity. To this question, then, of the role of ethical principles in developing partnerships, we will turn in the next chapter.

COMMENTARY ON READINGS

1. *Primary Sources*

Erikson, Erik: In several of his recent works Erikson has begun to elaborate a model of ethical behavior which is inspired by psychoanalytic theory and practice. The focal value of this system is the development of mutuality among partners. Especially helpful are the following:

Insight and Responsibility. New York: W.W. Norton, 1964. Cf. especially ch. VI, "The Golden Rule in the Light of the New Insight."

Gandhi's Truth. New York: W.W. Norton, 1969. By recreating the context of an early Gandhian confrontation, in which he first employed the fast as a political tool, Erikson seeks to interpret the personality of the Mahatma and to illustrate the meaning of mutuality as a moral paradigm.

Freire, Paulo: *The Pedagogy of the Oppressed*. Translated by M.B. Ramos. New York: Herder & Herder, 1970. A synthesis of ethics, pedagogy and politics.

Niebuhr, H. Richard: The late Professor of Christian Ethics at Yale has proposed the most revolutionary theory of morality to appear in America. For development of themes found in this essay, cf. especially:

The Responsible Self. With an Introduction by James M. Gustafson. New York & Evanston: Harper & Row, 1963.

The citation from Niebuhr in this chapter is taken from: *The Purpose of the Church and Its Ministry.* New York, 1956. Written in collaboration with Daniel Day Williams and James M. Gustafson, who is Niebuhr's most distinguished commentator. The citation is found on p. 35.

Thoughtful commentaries on the ethics of Niebuhr will be found in *Faith and Ethics: The Theology of H. Richard Niebuhr.* Edited by Paul Ramsey. Torchbooks. New York: Harper & Row, 1957.

Rogers, Carl: *Becoming Partners: Marriage and Its Alternatives.* New York: Delacorte, 1972.

Rogers does not explicitly mention ethical theory, but presents rich and provocative reflections on the significance of partnership as a mode of interpersonal existence. Cf. especially ch. 9, "Threads of Permanence and Enrichment."

Winter, Gibson: The Professor of Christian Ethics at the University of Chicago has presented a subtle and comprehensive ethical vision congenial to the thought of H. Richard Niebuhr. His works include:

Elements for a Social Ethic. New York: Macmillan, 1966.

Love and Conflict. Dolphin Books. Garden City: Doubleday, 1961

Being Free. London: Collier-Macmillan, 1970.

2. *Supplementary Readings*

Bultmann, Rudolf: *History and Eschatology, The Presence of Eternity*. Torchbooks. New York & Evanston: Harper & Row, 1957.

Jesus and the Word. Translated by L.P. Smith and E.H. Lantero. New York: Charles Scribner's Sons, 1958.

Kerygma and Myth. Edited by H.W. Bartsch and translated by R.H. Fuller. Torchbooks. New York: Harper & Row, 1961.

Primitive Christianity and Its Contemporary Setting. Translated by R.H. Fuller. Cleveland & New York: Meridian, 1956.

Cenkner, William: "Gandhi and Creative Conflict." *Thought*, XLV, no. 178 (Autumn, 1970), 421-32.

Deutsch, Karl: *Nationalism and Its Alternatives*. New York: A. Knopf, 1969.

Dubarle, A.M.: *Le Péché originel dans l'Ectiture*. Paris: Cerf, 1958.

Kuhn, Thomas S.: *The Structure of Scientific Revolutions*. Phoenix Books. Chicago & London: University of Chicago, 1964.

Ligier, Louis: *Péché d'Adam et Péché du monde*. Lyons: Aubier, 1960. On the subject of risk and the human predicament, cf. especially pp. 199-228.

Samartha, Stanley: "Mahatma Gandhi: Non-Violence and the World of Conflict." *Journal of Ecumenical Studies*, VII, 1 (Winter, 1970), 52-60.

Thakur, Shivesh: "Gandhi's God." *International Philosophical Quarterly*, XI, 4 (Dec. 1971), 485-95.

Thayer, Frederick: *An End to Hierarchy! An End to Competition!* New York: New Viewpoints, 1973.

Troeltsch, Ernst: *The Social Teaching of the Christian Churches*, I, II. Translated by Olive Wyon. Torchbooks. New York: Harper & Brothers, 1960. The citation in this chapter is from II, 1012.

2. Principles

The central insight of contextualist ethics, as described in the previous chapter, is the primacy of social process in determining moral choices. Because of the complexity of the human situation and because people approach moral dilemmas with a variety of principles which are themselves often mutually contradictory, contemporary thinkers suggest that social process must become the final arbiter of choice. By immersing oneself in the give-and-take of daily living, one is able to discern which of the competing moral claims is appropriate to the present moment. Social conflict selects the relevant value and points toward the fitting response in the situation. Commitment to social process is the final principle of morality.

What is the validity of this contemporary model of decision-making? Can the ideal of partnership replace the various ethics of principles? Can society safely abandon its armory of absolute norms and rely simply on social interaction to enlighten the perplexed conscience of modern man? Is it true to say that process is the principle?

We indicated earlier that the great persuasiveness of the contextualist approach to ethics stems from its recognition that almost all significant human activity consists in some process of sharing. At the same time, however, it was suggested that the simple reliance on social process as a moral norm was inadequate. In this chapter we will support this qualification of contextualist ethics by pointing out that social process itself relies on the constant observance of certain patterns of behavior. We will, then, be reflecting here on the dialectic of principle and process in moral reasoning.

Contextualist ethicians, such as H. Richard Niebuhr, have persuasively argued that most profound human experience consists in communication—a sharing among individuals. For this reason they insist that moral principles be understood within this perspective of partnership or social process. What they have been less successful at is uncovering the precise relationship between principles and social process. In the pages which follow we will explore this question of the role of moral principles in the ongoing process of communication.

Adherence to principles is an inherent element in all successful partnerships. We defined partnership earlier as a relationship of mutual dependence and reciprocal influence between two (or more) independent personal sources of initiative. Without a foundation of genuine self-respect, no one is able to be a partner to another. Before mutual dependence can occur there must exist two autonomous individuals. Otherwise, partnership will be replaced by absorption or domination of one person by the other. Another way of describing this prerequisite of independence is to speak of the person's principles—things that the individual would resist doing, even at the expense of the partnership itself. There must be an identity, and therefore clearly defined limits to a person's range of choices, before there can be a sharing of identities. In the most general sense, then, the adherence to moral principles can be described as one of the psychological systems which govern the fusion of individual initiative with social assimilation. Principles are a psychological prerequisite of social process.

Truthfulness is an obvious example of a moral principle which is implied by the ideal of partnership, but which logically stands outside the process itself as a normative or governing consideration. Perhaps it took the Watergate scandal, or at least the recent studies of governmental decision-making in the Vietnamese conflict, to remind us of the indispensability of truth-telling in any social process. David Halberstam's study of the Vietnam tragedy, *The Best and the Brightest*, traces the pattern of deception that prevailed in government circles during this period. His stark conclusion is that politically motivated deception (of the United States public and our allies) finally came full circle when the authors of the deception were duped by the reports circulated within the government itself. Hannah Arendt also comments on the irony that the President finally became the last one to learn the facts of the situation. The processes of government collapsed when lying became standard operating procedure in the bureaucracy.

In quite another sphere of life, the affective relationships of couples, Carl Rogers has discovered a similar rule: that permanent and enriching relationships depend on the consistent observance of truthfulness between partners. Writing, in *Becoming Partners*, of his study of a variety of personal relationships, Rogers claims that one of the four constant elements in all the *successful* partnerships he discovered was this commitment by each partner:

I will risk myself by endeavoring to communicate every

present feeling, positive or negative, to my partner. . . .
Then I will risk further by trying to understand, with all
the empathy I can bring to bear, his (or her) response. . . .

Truthfulness among the partners to any social process,
public or private, is the first principle of partnership.
No reliance on social process will be justifiable unless
this *norm* of behavior is observed. We see, then, that
the process itself of partnership implies the commitment to a moral principle which is, at least logically, independent of the social process. Another way of expressing this view is that the commitment to social
process must add the qualifying expressions "truthful"
or "honest" or "totally communicative" to social process if it is not to be abortive. Not every social process,
then, merits unqualified reliance or unquestioned commitment, but only those processes based on open communication.

   This qualification of contextualist ethics by the addition of the principle of truthfulness suggests the need
to establish some criteria for *assessing* social processes
before relying on them to reveal moral solutions. The
necessity to discriminate among social processes before
relying on them as moral guides is a central motif of
the natural law tradition in ethical theory. It would not,
I think, be an exaggeration to claim that the basic insight of this moral doctrine is precisely the opposite of
the newer moral model of contextualism. While the
contextualist (such as H. Richard Niebuhr) insists that
moral principles may be misleading and that social process winnows the irrelevant principles from the relevant
ones, natural law thinkers claim that social processes
are often misleading and that it is the role of principles

to discern between adequate and inadequate social systems. One can hardly imagine a clearer or more irreconcilable division between schools of thought than this clash.

The historical origins and periodic renewal of natural law thinking tend to support the claim that the doctrine emerges into relevance whenever people are faced with the simultaneous and competing claims of contradictory social systems, or when the single prevailing social structure comes into conflict with the inner convictions and social needs of individuals. It is precisely to choose between alternative social models, or to resist the encroachments of the only available, but uncongenial, social context that the natural law theory is useful. For example, the origins of the theory are traced to the inter-cultural clashes experienced by sixth century (B.C.) Athenians when they encountered nearby flourishing cultures based on alternative myths, religions and legal systems. Under the impact of the cross-cultural awakening, and stimulated by some of the social inequalities of Athens, itself, such as the denial of citizenship to non-Athenians, various Sophists began to question the moral validity of Athenian customs and laws, contrasting them with a law of nature, that is, a more equitable and reasonable law, not created by legislation but found written in the structure of reality. The theory originated as a critical approach to positive law, exposing its arbitrariness and challenging its authority. Under the pressure of skeptical questioning, Athenian society began to question itself and later to formulate the philosophy of law illustrated in the Platonic dialogues. This theory of natural law assimilated the critical insight of the Sophists without endorsing the lawlessness which it seemed to imply. In the *Republic*

we find the results of this synthesis which recognized
the natural basis (and therefore moral authority) of
good laws while rejecting the pretensions of legal absolutism.

The critical distinction between good and bad laws,
based on the conformity of positive law to some eternal, supra-legal standard, has remained as the corner-
stone of natural law thinking and has accounted for its
perennial revival during and following periods of social
crisis, when normal social structures prove inadequate
to govern the community. For example, the horrors
which were perpetrated by both sides during World
War II gave rise to a renaissance of natural law thinking at mid-century, which is reflected in Heinrich Rommen's *The Natural Law*. Rommen, himself a German
lawyer and an exile from Hitler's Germany, repeats the
ancient lesson: there are political regimes which so contradict profound human instincts that the citizen is
obliged to resist them.

Rommen, although he spent his last 30 years in
America, probably was not acquainted with the contextualist ethics of H. Richard Niebuhr. If he had been,
however, he probably would have viewed Niebuhr's
Responsible Self as historically naive. Undoubtedly, no
one who had been forced to flee his homeland could
have written with Niebuhr's assurance that social process can serve as a final arbiter among competing principles. Niebuhr's own lifelong experience of reliable social structures in the United States profoundly
influenced his own inclination to rely on the political
processes of adjudication among competing claims.
Niebuhr's "social existentialism" is, after all, a distinc-
tively American creation both in fact and in spirit. It
leaves unanswered the deeper questions of a conscience

caught in a society inimical to man. There is no room in Niebuhr for total resistance to society. He leaves too little ground for the individual to stand upon in fidelity to conscience. This lacuna in Niebuhr's contextualism reveals once more the indispensability of some moral principles by which an individual can pass judgment on the social processes in which he is involved. Principles are a necessary complement to partnership as a moral paradigm.

But precisely which principles? The contextualists, after all, are right when they claim that principles themselves are often in conflict with one another and that moral absolutes can breed moralistic absolutism. Although principles are tools to facilitate the articulation of individual identity and social assimilation, in fact they often alienate a person from his society and, with almost equal frequency, even from himself, from his deepest feelings and personal convictions. A person's principles can make his partnership with others almost impossible.

We have then to reflect further on the function (and dysfunction) of principles in the social dynamics of partnership. For the sake of such reflection, let us examine an hypothesis, namely, that moral principles can serve a useful function as social symbols to correlate the activities of large numbers of people who seek to live peacefully and securely within a complex social system. According to this hypothesis, principles consist in rational or legal statements of expected social behavior, which are useful because they are: unambiguous (and therefore easy to grasp), and substantially equitable (and therefore capable of winning wide acceptance and generating broad observance). As cultural symbols such moral principles are not antithetical to the processes of partnership in a society, but constitute one of the communication systems which allow a society to function. For example, the prohibition against killing except in self-defense is a social convention which curbs potentially destructive activity and allows individuals to live in relative security. Residents of some major American cities are beginning to experience for the first time the insecurity of living in a society where this convention is not observed. Without some broadly accepted restraints on individual behavior, the higher functions of life become impossible. Political society aspires to much greater benefits than security, but it cannot function in an atmosphere of fear.

Basic moral principles, which find their way into laws, express unconscious agreement by a society to the observance of certain symbolic boundaries between individuals and groups. The transgression of such boundaries, if unchecked, gradually unravels the fabric of a society. Principles are, in other words, one of the constitutive elements of political partnership. An ethics of partnership, therefore, cannot ignore or deny the validity of principles without giving rise to forces liable to overwhelm the fragile structure of society.

If this hypothesis is correct, and if society cannot function without consistent observance of the basic moral principles enshrined in its legal system, why is there such resistance in contemporary thought to the notion of ethical principles? Here let me suggest another hypothesis about the function of principles, or rather, about their dysfunction. The hypothesis was hinted at above in the original description of principles as social symbols designed to correlate the activities of *large numbers* of people seeking to live peacefully and securely within a *complex social system*. In this definition, there is stress laid on the number of people whose activity is supposed to be coordinated by acceptance of the legal symbol. Specifically, the definition supposes that principles are regulators of *political* activity, that is, of *public* activity involving *many individuals unknown* to *each other* and therefore *not personally responsive* to *one another*. Principles in this sense (and their embodiment in laws) were never meant to regulate the private behavior of a few individuals in face-to-face relationships with one another. This illegitimate extension of the notion of legal principles to purely private behavior may have been one of the truly monumental errors of moral and legal philosophy. The contemporary rejection of moral principles may well be due to a deep sense of the inappropriateness of ethical language which speaks of intimate inter-personal activity, such as sexual encounter, in political terms. The classical natural law language concerning sexuality is a glaring example of an ethical theory which fails to recognize the obvious distinction between the political and private spheres of life. One illustrative example is the scholastic terminology for sexual intercourse, which is spoken of as: "rendering the marriage debt." Not only is the language offensive but, more importantly, the categorical confusion behind the language is a theoretical error as well.

In the interest of recapturing the original inspiration of the Greek theory of natural law, it is tempting to return to the Athenian world view which equated human freedom (and ethics) with politics, while relegating family life to the area of human necessity. For the Athenian, since personal relationships were not a matter of free choice but of destiny, decisions in this sphere were not considered a legitimate part of ethics. While our own traditional perspective unhappily ignores the gulf between the political and private sectors of life and thereby confuses the notion of principle, it would not be wise to return completely to the Greek view. These two spheres of life are quite disparate. Yet there remains an *analogy* between the political and inter-personal spheres of activity. It is this *analogy* that should be stressed in the current renewal in moral theology, with equal attention being paid to the points of similarity and of difference between public and private existence. Both sectors of life are partnerships and so contain elements of similarity to one another. But the types of partnership differ profoundly. For our purposes of ethical analysis, the difference may be expressed by saying that political association is a partnership which, due to the complexity of the social organization, depends on the observance of laws and general moral principles in order to flourish, while familial relationships are constituted by partnerships which can prescind from all general rules (except the principle of honest communication) and rely on the inter-personal dynamics of affective communication to direct their course.

Collegial Wisdom

If the hypotheses argued above are accepted, and if one therefore admits a role for general moral and legal principles as a method of communication among the partners involved in complex and public social relationships, one must go on to ask *how* these principles facilitate "political" partnerships. By analyzing further the notion of principles as symbolic coordinators of activity for large aggregates of individuals in a social system, we hope to indicate that principles function as guidelines of activity to be applied or modified in individual instances by the exercise of individual and collective *judgment*. Prudence, in other words, which is defined by St. Thomas as the application of moral principles to concrete decisions, is the human activity through which principles can promote partnership.

Recent Thomistic scholarship has shed light on the centrality of prudence in the thought of St. Thomas. Specifically, Josef Pieper in his essay on "Prudence" and John Courtney Murray, S.J., in his book *We Hold These Truths*, have both emphasized that St. Thomas had a profoundly different view of the utility of principles than most of his modern followers. Pieper and Murray do not remark on the fact, but it is quite likely true that St. Thomas' view also differed from most other contemporary advocates on the ethics of principles as well, for Thomas viewed moral principles as a *tool* to be *applied* by *individual judgment*. For him, general statements about moral value (except for the most abstract principle of "doing good and avoiding evil") were simply instrumentalities of human wisdom, a starting point for the discernment process engaged in by the few persons who could be called "wise." On this point, Thomas rejoined the Platonic tradition in reserving specific moral judgment to a select few, distinguished for their knowledge of human affairs and their own rectitude. The very complexity of the human condition, Thomas argued, made it impossible for the average person to decide which moral principle applies in a given situation.

We will postpone for a later discussion the Thomistic notion of wisdom and the essentially authoritarian or hierarchical bias implied in this notion, for a contemporary emphasis on collegiality throws into doubt the current relevance of Thomas' elitism of moral insight. Here we will only reflect on some of the reasons *why* he reserved final judgment to a few.

St. Thomas' skepticism about the futility of seeking to enunciate self-applying formulas of value may have arisen from the very nature of moral principles as symbolic coordinators of social activity. It will be evident upon reflection that a symbol, which can appeal to a large aggregate of people and so serve as an agreed upon boundary of activity, must of its very nature be easily recognizable and, therefore, unambiguous. It must be couched in very general terms such as: "no killing except in self-defense." If the principle were formulated more precisely, it would cease to serve as a symbol and thus would lose its effectiveness as a means of social coordination. In short, a moral principle, as a social symbol, is a blunt instrument. It cannot of itself cut clearly to the final decision. For this reason, there are no self-applying formulas of value. To lead to a good practical judgment, a moral principle must be employed by a skilled interpreter, one who knows both the principle and the facts of the specific case. Moreover, the interpreter must be able to judge somewhat intuitively the connection between principle and fact. Such a person is described by St. Thomas as "a wise man." Moral principles are not self-applying formulas of value but symbols to be employed by a skilled artist of the moral life, a sage.

While a modern moralist is inclined to agree with St. Thomas on the futility of searching for self-applying formulas of value, there would be serious doubt registered now about the Thomistic solution offered by the solitary sage. The reasons for these hesitations are obvious enough and can best be summarized by asking the question: "Who in fact are these wise men in our culture whom we would trust to direct our lives? To whom should we turn?"

Even if two or more of us could agree on the designation of such wise men, it would not solve the problem of political ethics as defined above. For moral dilemmas in the field of complex social relationships involve large aggregates of individuals. In our pluralistic culture, there simply is no one or no group who could be agreed upon as final arbiter of morality. There is no practical way of selecting the wise men to make the final and decisive nexus between principles and specific solutions. And so, as the scholastics used to say, "ruit systema" ("there goes the show"). We must look for another way of arriving at moral insight.

That alternative approach to locating moral wisdom in a pluralistic culture is collegiality—the reliance on the potential creativity of conflicting minds in search of a solution. Not a wise man, but society itself, which Murray used to define as "men locked together in argument" is the reservoir of wisdom. This shift from Murray's reliance on the sagacious individual (a reliance which accorded nicely with a monarchical model of authority) to the contemporary emphasis on communal discernment and collegiality is manifested by reflecting on Murray's own definition of wisdom as "a care that is not an interest." There may have been a time and a culture which believed in the possibility of such disinterested concern. In our time and place we do not. Much closer to contemporary convictions on the possibility of arriving at moral insight is the acceptance of the principle of creative conflict among all the interested parties to a decision. Today we are more inclined to think that if all the interested parties are given a genuine voice, the final word will be as close to the practical truth as we can come.

The renewed emphasis on collegiality in the church is a recognition of the indispensability of including in the decision-making process all the interested parties to the decision. In secular American society, the renaissance of constitutionalism in the wake of Watergate represents a similar conviction that political truth is arrived at only by fostering the ordered conflict among the branches of government. Without conflict, the truth will continue to escape us. Wisdom, in other words, is a communal possession which we can attain only through the exercise of political partnership.

Even those who tentatively adopt the paradigm of partnership as the most adequate interpretation of the moral life must conclude, in the light of these reflections, that all *political* partnerships rely on the observance of moral principles, because they serve to regulate and coordinate the activities of large aggregates of people. The consistent violation of basic principles, such as the right to life, to assemble or to worship, can be taken as a warning to individuals not to rely on established social processes for guidance. When these basic rights are ignored, political partnership has collapsed and the individual must locate or construct some alternative social system within which to seek the truth. Social processes themselves must be subjected to the test of principles: Does the society (government, school, church, etc.) accept and observe the social symbols enshrined in the law? If so, then the individual may largely commit himself to the society as a moral guide. If not, he must become a rebel. In the following chapter we will reflect further on the suffering and tension involved between maintaining personal integrity and achieving social assimilation. To do so we will employ Camus' image of morality as rebellion. In this way we will complete our meditation by locating the phenomenon of morality within the context of the great mysteries surrounding life: the cross of Jesus, the future promised to mankind and the fundamental partnership between God and man which is realized in prayer.

COMMENTARY ON READINGS

Arendt, Hannah: *Crises of the Republic*. Harvest Books. New York: Harcourt, Brace, Jovanovich, 1972. The volume includes essays of importance on "Lying in Politics," "Civil Disobedience," and "On Violence." (Some similar reflections appeared earlier in "Truth and Politics," *The New Yorker*, Feb. 25, 1967, pp. 49-88.)

Eichmann in Jerusalem. Compass Books. New York: Viking Press, 1965. Ms. Arendt makes some intriguing observations on the function of social symbols (boundaries) in protecting or betraying Jewish communities during this tragic period.

Gustafson, James: *Christ and the Moral Life*. New York & Evanston: Harper & Row, 1968. This magistral survey of Christian ethics covers most of the themes of the present essay.

"Context versus Principles: A Misplaced Debate in Christian Ethics." *Harvard Theological Review*, LVIII, 2 (April, 1965), 171-202.

Halberstam, David: *The Best and the Brightest.* New York: Random House, 1972.

Murray, John Courtney, S.J.: *We Hold These Truths.* New York: Sheed & Ward, 1960. Cf. especially chs. 4, 8, 12.

Pieper, Josef: "Prudence," in *The Four Cardinal Virtues.* Notre Dame: University of Notre Dame, 1966, pp. 3-40.

Rogers, Carl: *Becoming Partners: Marriage and Its Alternatives.* Cf. observations following the previous chapter.

Rommen, Heinrich: *The Natural Law.* Translated by T.R. Hanley. St. Louis: Herder & Co., 1947. Cf. especially chs. I, IX, XII, XIII, XIV.

Schelling, Thomas: *The Strategy of Conflict.* London & New York: Oxford University Press, 1960. The *analogous* functions of moral principles and topographical boundaries as social coordinators occurred to me while reading Schelling's analysis of international strategies from the perspective of game theory. Schelling's own preoccupation, however, is not with ethical theory.

Winters, Francis X., S.J.: Some reflections on the role of moral principles in political decision-making appear in:

"A Rule of Thumb for Politicians." *America*, vol. 123, 1 (July 11, 1970), 11-12.

"The Wake in Washington." *America*, vol. 128, 13 (April 7, 1973), 302-04.

3. Mystery

The decisive symbol of successful partnership is the cross. For Christians there can be no hope of enjoying a life unmarred by failure. And yet the fundamental moral attitude of Christians remains that of magnanimity—the relentless effort to care for the whole creation, to shape the world into a more fitting habitation for humanity. This paradoxical combination of lofty aspirations and the realistic anticipation of personal defeat is the mysterious context in which mankind lives out its moral life. In this theological chapter we will reflect further on the implications of the mysterious partnership between God and man which is at once man's dignity and his tragic destiny. Our reflections will focus on suffering, on prayer and on hope.

Suffering

It is illusory to expect harmony between the individual's moral instinct and society as he finds it. The history of conscience is a story of resistance, of tension between the sense of integrity and the demands of society. It is perhaps for this reason that the great heroes of the spirit so frequently meet the fate of a martyr. Christ, Socrates, Thomas More and Gandhi all illus-

51

trate the deep antagonism between the good man and the world in which he lives. Conscience is at odds with the world.

Albert Camus experienced this opposition so deeply that he came finally to define the moral man as a rebel. Convinced that rebellion is one of the essential dimensions of man, Camus describes at length the phenomenon of resistance which he places at the source of conscience.

What is a rebel? A man who says no. . . . What does he mean by saying "no"?

He means, for example, that "this has been going on too long," "up to this point yes, beyond it no," "you are going too far," or again, "there is a limit beyond which you shall not go." In other words, his no affirms the existence of a borderline. . . . In a certain way [his no] confronts an order of things which oppresses him with the insistence on a kind of right not to be oppressed beyond the limit that he can tolerate. (*The Rebel*, p. 13)

If Camus is right, the touchstone of morality is conflict, the unending struggle to establish the legitimate boundary between personal identity and social assimilation. According to this view, one can detect the presence of morality in his life by asking himself: "What am I resisting? Where are the lines of the struggle in my life?" Conscience is the capacity to rebel.

In another essay, "The Myth of Sisyphus," the author makes it clear that this struggle is not one of the phases of the moral life, but simply a description of morality itself. The ancient myth of the hero destined to roll a rock up an ascending slope, only to see it ever roll down again, is not merely a story from the past—it is a symbol of mankind at all times. Futility is his fate, yet Sisyphus is content.

> I leave Sisyphus at the foot of the mountain! One always finds one's burden again. . . . The struggle itself toward the height is enough to fill a man's heart. One must imagine Sisyphus happy. (*The Myth of Sisyphus*, p. 91)

Painting the same picture in his novel, *The Plague*, Camus concludes the tale of a doctor's battle against an outbreak of the plague with these reflections on the hero, Dr. Rieux:

> Nonetheless, he knew the tale he had to tell could not be one of final victory. It could be only the record of what had had to be done, and what assuredly would have to be done again in the never ending fight against terror and its relentless onslaught, despite their personal affliction, by all who, while unable to be saints but refusing to bow down to pestilence, strive their utmost to be healers. (*The Plague*, p. 278)

Here is the modern voice of the moralist, who himself took his place in the French Resistance during the German occupation. One feels that Camus would rewrite the traditional maxim of moral philosophy: "do good and avoid evil" by urging us to "do good and resist evil."

A contemporary dramatist, Robert Bolt, who admits the influence of Camus' philosophy on his own work, has a similar perspective on the inevitability of conflict between conscience and the demands of society. In the preface to his drama *A Man For All Seasons*, based on the life of Thomas More, Bolt wonders aloud about his selection of More as a hero. The author concludes that More's appeal stems from his possession of integrity—the capacity to say "no" and to stick by it. Comparing contemporary society to the modern city, Bolt remarks:

. . . it is with us as it is with our cities—an accelerating flight to the periphery, leaving a center which is empty when the hours of business are over. . . . (*A Man For All Seasons*, p. xi)

We feel—we know—the self to be an equivocal commodity. There are fewer and fewer things which, as they say, we "cannot bring ourselves" to do. We can find almost no limit to ourselves. . . . (*A Man For All Seasons*, p. xii)

Because of the vacuum which has replaced moral rigor in modern society, More became for Bolt a striking hero of selfhood.

At any rate, Thomas More, as I wrote about him, became for me a man with an adamantine sense of his own self. He knew where he began and where he left off, what area of himself he could yield to the encroachments of his enemies, and what to the encroachments of those he loved. It was a substantial area in both cases, for he had a proper sense of fear and he was a busy lover. Since he was a clever man and a great lawyer, he was able to retire from these areas in wonderfully good order, but at length he was asked to retreat from that final area where he located his self. And there this supple, humorous, unassuming and sophisticated person set like metal, was overtaken by an absolutely primitive rigor, and could no more be budged than a cliff. (*A Man For All Seasons*, p. xi)

The common fate of Socrates, More and Gandhi is not merely a striking convergence of exceptionally tragic outcomes. It reveals a fundamental law: that conflict is the sign of genuine conscientiousness. Gandhi expressed the law in a letter to his followers: "We must be prepared for mountains of suffering."

Jesus was no exception to this rule. Rather, at least for Christians, his death on the cross is the eternal event that validates the law of suffering. His death is normative for all human life and says the final "no" to all human longing for personal success and continual comfort. It is the death of Jesus which is the decisive symbol of morality.

In *The Politics of Jesus*, John Yoder has explored this theme from the perspective of a pacifist. Yet, his exegetical and theological reflections have relevance for other moral options as well. Setting the persecution and killing of Jesus within its political context, Yoder traces his death to the unacceptability of Jesus' message that salvation was intended for Gentiles as well as Jews. This "heretical" claim to universalism was at once an inevitable conclusion from the fact that salvation is from God, the father of all men, and a frontal assault on the entire Jewish religious heritage, which was exclusivistic. By continuing to preach this message in the face of threats and of opposition, Jesus made his own death inevitable. But to restrict his message of universal salvation would have been to betray his Father. And so Jesus, by virtue of his commission to preach the good news, was set on a collision course with his own society.

The point of Yoder's book is the *normative* role of Jesus' death in the life of the believer. No Christian can expect to escape the fate of Jesus, which was to be at odds with his world. Not every follower of Jesus will die for his convictions, but persecution will certainly be his lot, for the universal message of salvation will always contradict some artificial boundary established by society, such as class, race, sex, or nationality. No one who, like Jesus, cares for the whole creation will be perfectly and permanently at ease in society.

The strange story told by the gospel is the incompatibility of genuine human achievement and personal success. Jesus' opposition to his society is the symbol of the tragic human condition, where each progression in understanding and sensitivity alienates the man of conscience from the conventional wisdom of his age. Since non-conformity is the fruit of conscience, every truly wise man will suffer the fate of Jesus, Socrates, More and Gandhi. While not every conscientious person will be a martyr, none will attain the success his talents seem to promise. All believers in the gospel will wear the sign of the cross.

Hope

There is a great temptation for Christians who take the cross seriously to forget about the empty tomb. Even deeply religious thinkers such as Rudolf Bultmann, who have understood the ruling symbol of the cross, are tempted to utter the blasphemy that the cross is final. Even Christians who accept the promise of overwhelming victory in Christ seem to be blinded by the futility of historical striving. Preachers of the passion of Christ often accept the tragic vision of existentialist thinkers such as Camus. In this admission of defeat, they underestimate the complexity of Jesus' meaning and undermine the Christian faith. The cross and the empty tomb together are the Christian symbols that interpret the human condition, not the cross alone.

There is no genuine Christianity without the experience of hope.

Hope denies the finality of futility and frustration, for it perceives that Jesus' resurrection, too, is precisely a *symbolic event*, an event that occurred to Jesus with the purpose of being extended to the life of every believer. When Jesus was raised, so were we all.

Hope, then, is a realization of the unequal but permanent partnership between God and man in caring for the universe. It senses that man has a real and indispensable role in governing the universe, which requires him to struggle continually to reform society without expecting to prevail. At the same time, hope knows that while God can and, in the present dispensation, must rely on man's efforts, He alone can bring these historical efforts to fulfillment in an order beyond time, in eternity. Hope is the Christian vision of the final age when human history will be transformed by the return of Jesus. Out of the permanent struggles of mankind and the partial fulfillment achieved by men and women, God will create the final reality, which will be a joint work of God and man. Teilhard de Chardin has expressed this vision by claiming that the whole course of history will serve God at the final moment of transformation as a rough-draft is used by an artist. History is the rough-sketch of God's kingdom, designed by mankind's painful labors and brought to fulfillment by the master's touch. Only with this final intervention will the myriad partial defeats of history be turned to a joint victory for God and man.

Hope moves beyond the mysterious futility of man's moral efforts in history to the deeper mystery of metahistory: the promise that God will make use of all these partial defeats to weave a permanent pattern of victory. Hope is an expression, then, of mankind's dignity as a moral agent and of his dependence on God to make sense of history. Denying the absurdist philosophy of existentialism, hope insists that a universe created by God cannot be without meaning. Any appearance of a law that sets power in a position of final victory over goodness is contrary to the claim that the world is created by a God who is wise, good and powerful. Hope, therefore, is simply the extension into the future of the act of faith—the acceptance of the fact of creation. Existentialists, who claim to accept the final absurdity of events, deceive themselves if they simultaneously claim to be Christians. One cannot *believe* in a God who dooms mankind to absurdity.

Prayer

It may seem strange in these days following the Second Vatican Council to preface a discussion of prayer with a review of the Council of Trent's doctrine of justification. It is, however, necessary, for a false understanding of the ravages of sin undermines the possibility of praying, and without the understanding of prayer there can be no genuine Christian morality. A brief delineation of what is meant here by the experience of prayer may help to explain the necessity for clarity in the Christian's understanding of nature and grace.

Personal prayer, as I understand it, is the *consciousness* of *partnership* with *God* in *caring* for the *universe*. Whether concomitant with one's daily work or in occasional quiet withdrawal from the fray, prayer tunes out the myriad details of acting and savors the meaning of what one is doing, the significance of the human task. In contrast to the current expression "consciousness-raising," which seems to consist in a process of choosing one's battleground, prayer is a process of consciousness-deepening, of coming into contact with the divine partner whose world one is helping to care for, and whose power alone can care for that world.

For those who are familiar with scholastic terminology, some reference to the relationship among providence, prudence and prayer may help to express this experience. In St. Thomas' theory of morality, prudence is the focus of the moral life because mankind's distinctive dignity consists in freely choosing his own future through the exercise of prudence. The gift of prudence, however, is the meeting place of divine and human activity, for prudence itself is man's self-activating share in God's rulership over creation (providence). What God accomplishes in the rest of creation through the fixed laws of nature, he allows to take place in man through his free exercise of choice. In a sense, God hands over to man the rulership of himself and of society. Prudence *is* God's providence for human society.

In this perspective, prayer is the *consciousness* of the *exercise* of *prudence*, including a sense of exhilaration at the use of such extraordinary powers. Prayer is the awareness that one is truly a partner with God in the governance of the world. Consequently, it is clear that this experience of prayer is incompatible with a widespread conviction, especially evident in Protestant theology from Luther to Reinhold Niebuhr, that all man's actions are vitiated by pride and self-seeking (original sin). It is not possible, logically or psychologically, to believe simultaneously that one is exercising God's own providence in caring for the world and that one is thereby sinning. Here finally one must choose between contradictory views of man. The Catholic vision affirms the dignity of man and insists that without the sense of inner worth man is unable to experience the destiny of partnership intended for him by God.

Prayer begins with the feeling of adequacy to meet the formidable challenge of sharing in the governance of the world. Before he can believe in the great mystery of morality: that human choice plays a constructive and even definitive role in the ongoing creation of the human universe, one must feel that his talents are equal to this task. Any theological world-view which identifies human activity with sin is bound to cut the nerve of morality by blurring the distinction between good and evil. If all human acts are sinful, why should one try to construct a theory of morality at all? Indeed, efforts at moral theology based on Lutheran pessimism, such as Reinhold Niebuhr's monumental synthesis, seem to verify the hypothesis that an affirmation of human dignity is the starting point of any viable ethical system.

It is characteristic and revealing that Reinhold Niebuhr defines prayer as repentance, the awareness in solitude that as soon as one acts, he sins. Between this absurdist vision, which denies the possibility of genuine human achievement, and the Catholic understanding of prayer as awareness of partnership with God, there is an unclosable chasm. At the very origin of Luther's reform, this division between contrary religious and philosophical perspectives was evidenced by Ignatius of Loyola, who inspired the Counter-Reformation. His little handbook of Christian living, *The Spiritual Exercises*, is built around the ideal of being a fellow-laborer with Christ (*collaborare cum Christo*). There is no way of avoiding this issue of human dignity. To deny it, as Neo-Orthodoxy has done, is to undermine the possibility of moral theology and, more fundamentally, to preclude the full experience of prayer.

Prayer, however, is more than a feeling of self-satisfaction. It is even more than the quiet experience of partnership with God, of being a fellow-laborer with Christ. Prayer opens up into hope, for an honest and thoughtful person shares with Niebuhr the awareness that his competence to care for the world is limited and fragmentary. He knows that the partial victories he achieves are seemingly outweighed by the setbacks on every side. And so the Christian at prayer immerses himself in the mystery of the end-time, when the resurrection symbolized by the empty tomb shall become a fact. Prayer is a religious consciousness which blends the sense of human dignity with the awareness of utter dependence on God, who alone will steal eternal victory from the jaws of historical defeat.

Nothing has been said yet of the primary form of Christian prayer, the Eucharist. Our remarks here will be confined to three dimensions of the liturgical experience: the Eucharist as the new covenant, as the sacramental symbol of Jesus' death and resurrection, and as the symbol of partnership among believers.

The significance of the Eucharist to the theme of this essay, partnership, is clear. The entire story of God's dealings with men, recounted in the Old Testament, can be summarized with the notion of testament itself, or covenant. It is only because of unfamiliarity with the notion of this covenant—a real and permanent partnership between God and his people—that we fail to be continually astonished by this revelation. A scandal to philosophy and a blasphemy to other religions, this theme of a covenant or relationship was renewed and transformed by the Lord's gift of his body and blood, which fulfilled the ancient promise of a new and interior covenant. In the Lord's supper there is a pledge of a union which is the central mystery of Christianity. Partnership is a contemporary expression for the ancient reality of a divine covenant with man, renewed daily in the Eucharist.

This special partnership requires on man's part the following of a certain way, the way of the cross. Suffering is the touchstone of man's fidelity to the covenant. In my own experience, this has been the central function of Christian worship, to place squarely before the eyes of the believer the symbol of the suffering Savior, to remind Christians that death is the law of life. Over the ages, despite vagaries of theological styles, and the varieties of liturgical forms, the centrality of the cross in Christian life has been insistently reiterated by the daily renewal of the Eucharist. By this showing forth of the death of the Lord *until he shall come*, the Christian is continually reminded as well of the empty tomb. Not merely the death of Jesus but his resurrection as well is signified by the Eucharist.

The symbolism of the Eucharist is not merely didactic, however, but sacramental as well. That is, the sharing of the Lord's supper brings about in the believer a continual conversion to the way of Jesus. The sacrament communicates the grace it symbolizes, namely, the transvaluation that differentiates genuine human achievement from mere success. No mere intellectual or even imaginative experience, but a taking on of the person of Jesus occurs in the Eucharist. In communion, the partnership of Lord and believer becomes actual.

Finally, it is of crucial importance to understand that the Eucharist is the Lord's *supper*. That is, believers go there together in order to express, to enact and to strengthen their covenant with one another. Symbolizing the fact that virtually all significant human activities arise from some sharing among individuals, the Eucharist itself is an act of partnership among members of the community of believers. In this act they share with one another their curious and nonconformist convictions and so ratify and deepen the partnership of resistance which is the church. By sharing in the mystery of the Lord's body, they become the mystery of the church. The Eucharist, then, is the prayer of the church *par excellence*, the prayer of God's community of partners in the task of caring for the creation.

COMMENTARY ON READINGS

Bolt, Robert: *A Man for All Seasons.* Vintage Books. New York: Random House, 1962. (For further reflections on Thomas More, cf. the graceful biography by R.W. Chambers, *Thomas More* [Ann Arbor Paperbacks. Ann Arbor: U. of Michigan, 1958]).

Bultmann, Rudolf: Cf. the titles listed after chapter 1.

Camus, Albert: "The Myth of Sisyphus," in *The Myth of Sisyphus and Other Essays.* Translated by J. O'Brien. Vintage Books. New York: Random House, 1955. Pp. 88-91.

The Plague. Translated by Stuart Gilbert. New York: Modern Library, 1948.

The Rebel. Translated by H. Read. Vintage Books. New York: Random House, 1956.

Council of Trent, The: Session VI (1547). In *Enchiridion Symbolorum.* Edited by H. Denzinger. Friburg: Herder & Co., 1937. Cf. the Decree on Justification, no. 792a-810, and the canons, no. 811-43, (pp. 284-89).

Documents of Vatican II: Translated and edited by Abbott and Gallagher. New York: America Press, 1966. Cf. "The Dogmatic Constitution on the Church," pp. 14-101.

Ignatius of Loyola: *The Spiritual Exercises.* Translated by T. Corbishley, S.J. New York: P.J. Kenedy & Sons, 1963.

Moltmann, Jürgen: *The Theology of Hope.* Translated by J.W. Laitch. New York & Evanston: Harper & Row, 1967.

Niebuhr, Reinhold: *Beyond Tragedy.* New York: Charles Scribner's Sons, 1937.

Faith and History. New York: Charles Scribner's Sons, 1949.

The Nature and Destiny of Man. Vol. I, II. New York: Charles Scribner's Sons, 1941, 1943.

(Cf. also John Courtney Murray's severe critique of Niebuhr's pessimism in *We Hold These Truths*, ch. 12, "The Doctrine Is Dead.")

Teilhard de Chardin, Pierre, S.J.: Teilhard's principal essays on ethics appear in volume 6 of his collected works: *L'Energie Humaine*. Paris: Seuil, 1962. (Eng. trans., *Human Energy*, [London: Collins, 1969]).

Yoder, John: *The Politics of Jesus*. Grand Rapids: Eerdmans, 1972.

Conclusion

The insight which inspired this essay is simple: that the secret to understanding morality lies in finding the correct starting point and that the proper starting point for ethical theory is not the individual but the relationship between or among individuals. To begin ethical reflection either with the self alone in focus or by looking only at the other person is to misconceive social reality as an *artificial* web of relationships which transiently unite individuals, who alone are thought to be *real*. Instead the moralist—and each of us as we reflect on the ethical quality of our lives—must always have at least two individuals in focus, for morality is not a quality of an individual person but of relationships among individuals. Ignoring this caution has led to the tiresome and fruitless debate between ethical theories based on self-interest and contradictory theories of altruism. In political philosophy, this endless debate is still heard between the power-brokers and the pacifists. Neither self-interest nor self-sacrifice can be ignored in morality, for both these attitudes are indispensable constituents of any healthy partnership, but one cannot start by isolating one or other of these attitudes and hope to construct a comprehensive theory of ethics. Rather one must start with the relationship itself and examine its quality. From there one can go on to inquire about the respective contributions of the two partners. The new imperative of partnership is proposed here in the belief that relationships are as real as persons and that the proper study of mankind is *man confronting man*.

The ethical question, then, is this: What is the quality of my relationships? Am I dependent on some others who in turn depend on me? Am I able both to respond to their initiatives and to create initiatives of my own? Do we both sometimes talk and sometimes listen? Do we complement one another? Do we also compliment and criticize one another? Does the relationship heighten the individuality of each and so enrich the relationship? Do we share some significant tasks such as spreading the gospel or raising a family? Are we partners?

If so, we undoubtedly make sacrifices for the sake of one another without compromising our own legitimate interests. Likewise we probably adhere to certain principles or recognizable patterns of activity, such as honest communication. We also experience continual movement in our relationship, and therefore never escape the necessity to risk what we have attained in order to maintain our relationship. To borrow Rogers' phrase, we are *becoming partners*.

All of these questions and affirmations seem to apply most aptly to intimate face-to-face relationships. On second thought, however, they can be applied analogously to the interaction of larger groups, even nations. Citizens and statesmen can examine their conduct toward other societies for the same qualities of interdependence, symmetry, reciprocity, complementarity. There is a genuine analogy of partnership which can serve as a paradigm of morality: a description of what is happening and a goal toward which to move.

But why bother with moral paradigms at all? What is the point of all this theoretical talk about how men choose? What good can come from ethical reflection? The answer to these questions is simple: the discovery that partnership is an image applicable to morality is the answer to a question that came unbidden into the mind of the author almost 20 years ago. Now he senses that many others are asking a similar question. Perhaps his answer will fit their question as well.

II
Politics

Introduction

An essay in ethical theory, such as the preceding one, is incomplete without an attempt to apply the theory to some practical moral dilemmas. To complete this analysis of the moral life under the rubric of partnership, then, an effort will be made here to test the theory's applicability to *political* decision-making. Three current questions will be addressed in turn: the Watergate scandal; the processes appropriate to determining national interests worthy of being pursued in American foreign policy (including specific reflections on the Vietnam experience); and, finally, the viability of the just war theory in the nuclear age. Each of these questions will be approached by asking what light the ideal of partnership might shed on the moral issues involved in these three areas of political life.

To highlight the theoretical question suggested in the opening essay, special attention will be devoted in each section to the complementary functions of the *process* of partnership and various moral *principles* which seem relevant to the respective issues. In each case it will be seen that, while the initiation and maintenance of partnership constitutes the fundamental principle, the implications of this imperative are spelled out in further moral principles, such as the necessity for reciprocal trust among partners, the need to extend the benefits of partnership beyond national boundaries, even to citizens of hostile nations in time of war.

1. Watergate

The proper starting point for settling questions of political morality is to search one's political heritage for a solution. Rather than looking immediately for moral norms as a guide, a citizen should inquire whether he may not find in the spirit of the laws of his nation the answer to his question. Only in rare instances is a citizen driven to rely on the transcendent standards of conscientious objection to the laws of his land. While many of our great political and moral heroes have been driven to challenge the entire political fabric of their nation, it would be misleading to regard the rebel as the exclusive model of political morality. For most citizens, the constitution of their state serves as an adequate moral standard because the moral values of a culture are normally recognized in its laws. Under most circumstances, the fundamental moral principle in politics is to observe the legal processes of one's nation. Thus, for citizens of the United States, the question of political ethics is simultaneously a constitutional question: Is the action under consideration constitutionally sanctioned or not? As the natural law tradition emphasized, even while it elaborated the exceptions to this rule, legal process usually coincides with moral principle.

Heinrich Rommen, in his study entitled *The Natu-*

ral Law (St. Louis: Herder, 1947), has clearly summarized this instinct of the natural law tradition to rely for moral guidance on positive legal codes of a nation.

The natural law . . . contains but a few universal norms and foregoes deductive extremes. It states explicitly that in the normative sciences certainty and necessity decrease in proportion as deduction moves farther away from the first self-evident principles. It has so strong a feeling for the great blessing of a secure and reliable legal order, which it considers a most essential element of the common good, that it regards as non-binding only that positive law which has been changed into non-law by the prohibitive norms of the natural law. . . . It is revolutionary only in respect to the law that has become materially immoral. Its attitude toward the imperfections of the positive law is merely reformist. It may with some exaggeration be called a skeleton law. It determines what positive arrangements, in themselves capable of being willed in given historical circumstances, can be right.

The natural law calls, then, for the positive law. This explains why the natural law, though it is the enduring basis and norm of the positive law, progressively withdraws, as it were, behind the curtain of the positive law as the latter achieves continually greater perfection. This is also why the natural law reappears whenever the positive law is transformed into objective injustice through the evolution and play of vital forces and the functional changes of communities.

Under constitutional government bulwarked by a Bill of Rights there exists indeed a strong presumption of law and of right that all laws enacted in keeping with constitutional procedure are not out of harmony with the natural law. It is from this assumption that such laws derive not only their factual enforceability but also their ultimate validity before conscience. (pages 251-61)

Political morality is embedded in one's political institutions. Only when these institutions themselves have failed to adapt to changing circumstances or when they have been maladministered is the conscientious citizen forced out onto the lonely path of seeking supra-political standards for behavior.

The moral force of the law stems from a conviction that the constitution safeguards and encourages a pattern of human relationship which is conducive to human welfare. The drafters of the United States Constitution, for example, believed that genuine and lasting political power is a product of partnership or voluntary association among citizens. That is, they judged that power is enhanced by diffusion throughout the society rather than by concentration in one person or body. By establishing a system of checks and balances among various groups, the founding fathers sought to ensure that authority would reside in the perpetually renewed *consent* of the people. Thus, they sought to protect the right of individuals to dissent from the majority, for it is out of the clash of conflicting opinion that consent must be continually refashioned. Basic to this philosophy of power is a profound trust in the collective wisdom of the people and a positive evaluation of social conflict as a source of unity and progress. For a citizen of the United States, then, political decisions are morally correct if they correspond to the prescribed patterns of partnership, which include the right to dissent from the opinion of the majority of one's fellow citizens, and to assemble with others of his own opinion. Dissent, individual and corporate, is a constitutive element of constitutional government and an exercise of the political partnership which is the constitutional ideal.

It is because the constitutionally established processes for achieving self-determination are indispensable means for fostering genuine political power that their observance is a matter of moral urgency. To violate these fundamental elements of the political heritage is to upset the proper functioning of political power, and hence to undermine the common good. Against this background, it is possible to attempt a moral assessment of the Watergate phenomenon.

Even a casual review of the origins of the United States Constitution reveals a deep resonance between its principle and the spirit of partnership, which was outlined in the preceding essay. The Convention which was held in Philadelphia to draft the Constitution met under a mandate to achieve a measure of political centralization among the Colonies which would not compromise their Revolutionary heritage of independence. Fresh from a military victory which had vindicated their claim to self-determination, the separate Colonies found that mere independence was not sufficient to ensure the peace and prosperity they had been seeking. Providing for the commercial, financial and diplomatic interests of the Colonies required some central coordinating body. What they desired was the capacity for concerted political action which would not be unilateral. The delegates thus convened under the complementary convictions that: (1) the people could not prosper without some concentration of power and (2) such power could not prosper without some effective internal restraint. Out of this search for self-limiting political organization emerged the Constitution, along with its Bill of Rights. Students of the Constitution point to the four-fold provisions for mutual restraint which appear in the document: the protection of individuals against other individuals, of individuals against the government, of state governments against the federal government, and of the three branches of the federal government against one another. This elaborate system of checks and balances embodies a philosophy closely akin to the model of partnership presented in our opening essay, for it allows and requires among the parties to the government a relationship of mutual dependence and reciprocal influence. No individual and no office holder is completely autonomous or completely subordinate. The Constitution might, then, be adequately described as a delineation of the process of political partnership. All unilateral decisions affecting the common weal are proscribed by the provisions of the document and are prevented as long as these provisions are observed.

How, then, have we arrived at Watergate? One can imagine that the arching eyebrows and outraged tones of Chairman Ervin would express the reactions of the signers of the Constitution if they were to listen to revelations of the same "horrors." What, as the Chairman kept asking in disbelief, ever became of the Constitution? A brief recapitulation of some political events—both foreign and domestic—which led up to Watergate may help to suggest the forces which have been operating for some time in the American people at cross-purposes to the Constitution.

The events which culminated in the Watergate affair can be traced back, I believe, to the Cambodian "incursion" of May 1970. The announcement of the invasion of this neutral nation shocked the Congress and stunned many Americans who had believed that the President was sincerely and effectively withdrawing from the war. Young people, in particular, were left reeling from the blow. Campus protests erupted spontaneously and, in the case of Kent State, tragically. The four killings at Kent State themselves deepened the feeling of powerlessness throughout the nation. The gloom which spread across the country happened to coincide with a rare celestial occurrence, an eclipse of the sun which was so complete along a certain path that cattle went to sleep as though night had fallen. Surely in a more primitive culture this coincidence would have been a fearsome portent of divine disfavor. In our own enlightened age we were able to direct our fears at that moment more rationally—to the unchecked and seemingly ungovernable usurpation of power by the Administration.

Reactions set in which, although they were unprecedented in United States history, could probably have been predicted. Campus after campus shut down, more out of shared confusion than with a positive purpose. Bombings followed in quick succession, culminating in the accidental explosion of an amateur bomb factory in a New York town house. Fear deepened.

The White House, which was by no means alone in its apprehension, began to fear for the fabric of the political system. Recalling Lyndon Johnson's expulsion from the Presidency by less dramatic protests, the Nixon Administration heightened its efforts—perhaps necessary and legitimate—to improve its intelligence capacity and enable it to prevent the spread of lethal violence. A "Special Investigation Unit" was formed to deal with the emergency.

In this sequence of events we see an action-response pattern consisting in: unilateral governmental action (Cambodian invasion), which generated a feeling of powerlessness on the part of the people, who responded in panic (Kent State), thus provoking further unilateral decisions by the government to control the violent reactions.

Another cycle of frustration, reaction and repression occurred when Daniel Ellsberg finally became disaffected with United States policies in Vietnam and decided to release portions of the Pentagon Papers to the press. Sensing his powerlessness, even as an influential citizen and consultant to the government, to bring about through normal procedures a cessation of hostilities, Ellsberg transmitted the study of the war to various newspapers and thus set off another series of special investigations and unilateral White House efforts to get control of the deteriorating domestic situation.

How would it have been possible for some of the principals involved in these incidents to have broken the chain of events that has brought the nation so low? How can we avoid Watergate Two?

At first glance, it appears obvious that the only villains in the piece were the Administration officials who were paraded before the Ervin committee. Surely these were the men responsible for the present state of affairs. If only they had taken the opposition seriously, confronting their political "enemies" openly rather than trying to subvert them, a more moderate course of action might have resulted. Watching the Committee witnesses and attending to their estimates of the atmosphere which prevailed in the White House, one is tempted initially to point to two attitudes on the part of the principals which precipitated the crisis: *fear* and *contempt*. Fear and contempt for their opposition. This apparently paradoxical blend of fear and contempt for the domestic enemies of Mr. Nixon provides a key to understanding the unconstitutional tactics employed in order to eliminate this opposition, for these attitudes, which reinforce one another, compelled the officials to avoid confronting their adversaries. Fear and contempt counseled subversion rather than open confrontation.

It is interesting to note that it was a British journalist, Henry Fairlie, who has perceived the essence of the political crisis instigated by Watergate. In an article which appeared in the *New York Times* on December 31, 1973, Fairlie observed:

The contempt for the people which has been demonstrated in the repeated disclosure of Presidential misconduct is only one reflection of a much wider and more general contempt for them which has been a part of the intellectual climate and political imagination of the United States for the last quarter of a century. The attitude has been that there is no help or hope in them. . . .

As the testimony before the Ervin Committee amply demonstrated, these were the almost unspoken, certainly unchallenged, assumptions of the White House under Richard Nixon and his senior aides. The despising of the democratic voter, and of the democratic process that is available to him, was instinctive. They simply had no sense of the "cherishment of the people" as the purpose of government. . . .

In return, the politicians and the commentators and the thinkers should seek to reinvest the estate with a public philosophy, at the center of which is a fundamental trust in the capacity of ordinary people to judge well and wisely in the long run between what is of lasting value and what is only meretricious.

It is tempting, then, to conclude that the present

crisis could have been avoided if only the Administration had been less fearful and more respectful of their opposition and had opened themselves to sustained confrontation with "the enemies" through the constitutional processes of political debate. This analysis is probably true as far as it goes. Yet it looks at only half of the political partnership which is the United States. It neglects to inquire into the responsibility of the opposition itself for some of the tragic events of the early '70s. The critics of the Administration, too, may have contributed to the unraveling of the political fabric. Perhaps they, too, were motivated by fear and contempt and so sought to subvert the Administration. Perhaps segments of the peace movement in their turn were unwilling to engage the Administration in a constitutionally sanctioned confrontation over the substantive policy issues. No effort seems to have been made by the peace movement for example to work through Congressional committees to end the war. It may be only a coincidence, but surely not one without symbolic significance, that the violation of private files was a tactic employed by both sides (Daniel Ellsberg as well as the "Plumbers Unit"). The preference for conspiracy over open confrontation was evident on both sides, and one might surmise that this preference arose from a mutuality of fear and contempt. Neither side appears to have been willing to engage the other in open, constitutional confrontation.

Political partnership is an ideal that rests on a positive view of social reality: that there exists in society as a whole the capacity to cope with its own future. On the basis of this faith, political partners claim for themselves and concede to others a "voice" in the determination of their common future: the right to speak, to be heard and to have one's interests considered. Sensing that it is as unhealthy to deny this "voice" to others as it is to be deprived of it oneself, political partners are patient in working out the shape of the future. For this reason they resist resolutely the effort to have the future determined by any one interest or any one insight.

The ideal of partnership is inextricably linked to the cultivation of complementary attitudes: self-respect and respect for others. It is striking that a review of the Watergate hearings highlights the influence of two attitudes diametrically opposed to this reciprocity of respect, namely, fear (stemming perhaps from lack of self-respect) and contempt. As we reflect on the relationship between the process of partnership and political morality, it is important to realize that no political process, such as the constitutionally defined political partnership of the United States government, can function automatically. Any political process is as strong as its acceptance by the citizens who live within it. Specifically, the U.S. governmental process is ineffectual and even dangerous if it is not animated by that mutual respect which constitutes the spirit of our laws. Political ethics begins with the political heritage of the country, both its constitutional formulation and its informing spirit. Political morality is the process of assimilating the spirit of one's political heritage and observing its formalities. Without the personal assimilation of "the spirit of the laws," observance of the laws themselves will surely wane.

The lesson of Watergate, then, is two-fold: (1) the surest guide to political morality is conformity to one's inherited political institutions, and (2) the surest way to guarantee this conformity is to recapture the political and moral vision which gave rise to these institutions originally. There is involved in the process of political renewal a return both to prescribed political process (obedience to the laws) and to the political principle (philosophy) which informs that process, namely, the principle of mutual respect and reciprocal influence. Perhaps, then, the distance between process and principle in political ethics is not so wide as it may sometimes appear.

2. National Interest and National Integrity

In discussing Watergate, it is important to dwell on the convergence between morality and legality which the Western tradition takes for granted under normal social circumstances. It is true, however, that any society must continually examine itself to determine whether it is extending its political benefits to all its members. Within the United States' experience, it is clear that the social history of the last 100 years can be read as the struggle to include within the living covenant of the Constitution all those citizens, including Blacks and women, whose nominal membership in the society has often been denied in practice since the beginning of the Republic. Political morality requires continuous scrutiny of the consistency and comprehensiveness of legal protection for all fellow citizens.

A more difficult question in political ethics, which cannot be resolved on legal grounds, concerns the relations among citizens of various nations or among nations themselves. Here no reliance on cultural and legal heritage is adequate to determine the morally correct choice among alternative courses of action. At the water's edge, the coincidence between the legal and moral order ceases. Political ethics, in other words, comprises two radically different questions: that of the regulation of domestic political affairs, where morality can usually be assumed to follow legality; and international politics, where there are virtually no legal solutions to moral dilemmas.

This profound difference between domestic and international issues in political morality has often enough gone unrecognized. As a result of this confusion, it has often been assumed that questions of ethics in international affairs can be adequately left to international lawyers or, conversely, that no discussion of ethics and international relations is possible because there is no comprehensive international law by which such questions might be resolved. Both of these positions assume an identity between legality and morality which obtains in the domestic situation but not in international affairs. Surely one of the most consistently fruitless controversies in intellectual history has arisen from this confusion—the "realist" versus "idealist" debate on ethics and foreign policy. A review of the latest round in this debate may highlight an area where the ethics of partnership might contribute to the advancement of political thought in America.

The latest engagements of the "realist" and "idealist" forces took place in the 1971 Christian Herter lecture series at the Johns' Hopkins School of Advanced International Studies and was published under the title: *Ethics and World Politics* (ed. E. Lefever). On this occasion, Arthur Schlesinger, Jr., defended the realist position while Senator Mark Hatfield attacked it from the perspective of an idealist. Paul Ramsey presented a middle position in the same debate.

Schlesinger, the American historian and former White House advisor, asked the question: "Should . . . overt moral principles decide issues of foreign policy?"

and replied: "Required to give a succinct answer, I am obliged to say: as little as possible." In defense of this position, which might be described as moral minimalism, Schlesinger points out—with striking inattention to the history of ethical thought prior to Twentieth Century American Protestantism—that ethics necessarily means self-sacrifice. Having asserted this dubiously historical identification of ethics and love, Schlesinger easily concludes that morality should be excluded from all save a few policy issues, which he calls "cases of last resort": "questions of war crimes and atrocities, of the nuclear arms race, of colonialism, of racial justice, of world poverty, and totalitarian aggression or repression" (Nazism and Stalinism). The reasons offered for exiling moral considerations to these areas of last resort include the standard argument: national leaders are trustees for the interest of the citizens, which they may not sacrifice to trans-national interests. Therefore, national interest alone should determine foreign policy, although in cases of last resort moral criteria may help to clarify and control the content of national interest. National interest, properly clarified, is thus seen as the ultimate criterion of foreign policy. Moral ideals serve otherwise only to promote fanaticism and undermine genuine national interest.

While Schlesinger makes national interest a virtually final criterion of foreign policy, Senator Hatfield conversely ignores national interest almost entirely in his analysis of the same problem. Resting his political judgments on the "ultimate worth of every individual human life" (regardless of nationality), Hatfield voices the widespread outrage at the excesses of recent American policy in Southeast Asia and insists that the validity of national interest as a criterion of policy has been discredited by recent history. In fact, he argues, "national interest" has been invoked by political leaders in such a way as to undermine our national integrity. In the name of national interest, citizens have been implicated in policy decisions which contradict their own sense of human dignity. Rejecting Schlesinger's "realist" approach to the problem, the Senator argues clearly for the reassertion of individual idealism and reverence for all human life.

Between these two contradictory claims for national interest or individual worth as criteria of foreign policy, no reconciliation seems possible. It seems after reading these two essays that the debate on ethics and foreign policy must go on unresolved. In the same lecture series, however, Paul Ramsey suggests an alternative approach to the problem which rejects the premises of both Schlesinger and Hatfield. Ramsey argues that the acceptance of either national interest or the worth of individual human beings is the wrong starting point for the argument. If the debate is framed in such terms, no resolution or even genuine confrontation is possible. In place of this formulation, then, Ramsey suggests focusing on the legitimate confrontation among competing national interests as the proper starting point of the debate. Rejecting Schlesinger's designation of the interests of the nation state as well as Hatfield's preference for the values of the individual person as ultimate criteria of policy, Ramsey accepts the legitimate claims of all national societies to formulate policy goals, but rejects the claim of such national interests to finality as criteria of policy. Rather, Ramsey locates morality in the acceptance by each nation and its leaders of the restraints imposed upon it by the legitimate claims and forces of competing nations. In the acceptance of such political confrontation lies the genuine moral instinct. Not the untrammeled national interest of, for example, the United States, but the clash of competing interests of various national actors constitutes the source of moral and political guidance. For Ramsey, then, force is a constitutive element in the achievement of morality in international affairs, since by enforcing its legitimate moral claims, a nation's leaders ensure that effective clash of interests that constitutes the common good of the international system.

It is apparent, I suppose, from this emphasis on the constitutive role of force in moral judgment that Ramsey's analysis of the relationship between ethics and foreign policy remains unfinished and in need of re-finement. While Ramsey has made an advance over the unilateral nationalism of Schlesinger and the atomistic individualism of Hatfield, he has not accounted in this essay for the right of weaker and poorer nations to assert their claim within the international system in default of comparable military force. Within Ramsey's argument there remains too large a role for brute strength: to some extent, Ramsey seems to imply that "might makes right." Even after Ramsey's perceptive intervention, the argument remains unfinished: how precisely can we relate ethics and foreign policy? What is the relation between national interest and national integrity?

There is an air of unreality surrounding this debate between the realists and their opponents. The entire discussion takes place in an ahistorical atmosphere, as though the three discussants were not fellow citizens of the United States and fellow heirs of a clearly defined political tradition within the Republic. Perhaps it would be possible, then, to refocus the argument by turning back to this specific political heritage within which all of the discussants live and by having them ask: What are the implications of the United States' domestic political heritage for its conduct of foreign affairs? How might *Americans* specifically shape their foreign policy?

In the discussion above of the constitutional crises provoked by Watergate, a brief sketch of the United States' political heritage was presented. Central to the constitutional heritage, in this interpretation, is the legacy of systematic procedures for reconciling conflicts of interest of various sectors of society. The Ervin Committee hearings revealed that it was precisely in the efforts to stifle such an anticipated conflict of views that "the plumbers" were organized. Public reaction to the illegality involved in the Watergate break-in was focused principally on the *intent* of the actors: to subvert dissent within the political process. The attempt to govern the Republic by silencing all voices but that of the President strikes at the very heart of the American political tradition for the American Constitution seeks to secure the common weal by arriving at a consensus which arises out of a free and open exchange of conflicting views. Each man and each interest are assured a voice in the shaping of this consensus. The Constitution enshrines the political philosophy which holds that power is enhanced by diffusion among various interests rather than by concentration in a single source.

Shifting our attention away from our current domestic difficulties once more, let us reflect on the implications of the constitutional heritage for United States' foreign policy. What kind of face must the United States wear toward the world if it is to be consistent with its own heritage? It should be obvious, I think, that the United States is committed to a certain set of goals and procedures in the international system by virtue of her own constitutional heritage. Perhaps Dean Acheson has expressed this as well as anyone in his reflections on the shaping of policy toward our NATO allies:

It has been the central idea of our nation, from the days of 1776 and earlier, that a free society is one in which diversity may flourish, in which the spirit of inquiry and of belief is free to explore and express. . . .

The spirit of free inquiry, free thought, is the kernel of what we are defending, and it is also the strongest weapon in our arsenal. What is more, it is the principal binding force in our coalition. The tradition of 1776 is still the most powerful and attracting force in the world today; it is this that draws to our leadership people all over the world. Without this idea, we are to them just another powerful nation, bent upon interests which are not theirs. If we are narrow, dogmatic, self-centered, afraid, domineering, and crabbed, we shall break apart the alliance on which our future depends. But, if we behave, in our dealings among ourselves and with our allies, as a free society should, we shall succeed in that most difficult task of leading a group of diverse peoples, doing unpleasant and burdensome things, over a long period of time, in the quiet defense of their precious liberty. It may be that this is the highest test of our American civilization which destiny has in store for us.

Interestingly, Arthur Schlesinger, Jr., in the same lecture under discussion here, makes much the same point about the necessity to achieve consistency between U.S. and domestic foreign policy:

The moral question arises particularly in a state's observance or non-observance of its own best standards. Foreign policy is only the face a nation wears to the world. If a course in foreign affairs implies moral val-

ues incompatible with the ideals of the national community, either the nation will refuse after a time to sustain the policy, or else it must abandon its ideals. A
people is in bad trouble when it tries to keep two sets of
books—when it holds one scale of values for its internal
policy and applies another to its conduct of foreign affairs. The consequent moral schizophrenia is bound to
convulse the homeland. This is what happened to
France during the Algerian war. It is what is happening
to the United States because of the Vietnamese War.

Later in the same talk, he comments further about the
tolerance implied by the very logic of national interest
itself:

The assumption that other nations have traditions, interests, values, rights, and obligations of their own is
the beginning of a true morality of states.

Acheson and Schlesinger are here suggesting that we
attempt to conduct foreign policy in the spirit of the
Constitution, that is, with the intention of allowing all
interested parties to have a voice in the determination
of decisions which affect their future. Such an approach
to foreign policy would suggest that the United States'
political heritage should serve as a moral norm for
United States' foreign policy. That is, United States
policy makers, convinced of the moral rectitude of their
own political philosophy, should seek to extend the benefits of that philosophy by contributing to the distribu-
tion of power throughout the international system. If it
is true, as the Constitution implies, that political power
is enhanced by diffusion rather than by concentration,
then it will be in the interest of the international common weal that as many nations as possible have a voice

in determining the shape of that international system. Our national integrity requires that our foreign policy be made consistent with our domestic political heritage by an effort to accept the validity of dissenting views of other nations and by seeking accommodation with these competing nations.

How does this analysis of the realist-idealist debate on ethics and foreign policy relate to the earlier discussion of the relationship between political process and moral principle in the formation of the conscience of a statesman or citizen? The formula proposed here for choosing among alternative courses of action on the basis of preferring those actions which help to diffuse power throughout the international system represents an effort to extend the insights of the U.S. domestic political heritage to our conduct of our foreign policy. In suggesting the criterion that no foreign policy decision should be inconsistent with the philosophy of power inherent in the U.S. Constitution, which holds that power is enhanced by diffusion rather than by concentration in a single point, there is operative the conviction that morality consists in extending as universally as possible to others the claims that one makes for himself. Political morality, in other words, is held to consist in the effort to universalize (apply to all others) the rights that one demands for oneself. If the United States claims self-determination as its own right (and as the right of each of its citizens), it is obliged for the sake of consistency to grant this same right of self-determination to all other nations which do not disqualify themselves as partners in the international political system by unjust or expansionist policies. Each nation in the international system is entitled to a voice in the settlement of issues in which it has a legitimate interest—the right to speak, to be heard, to have its interests considered.

Process and principle are related in this analysis as the particular relates to the universal. That is, the claim is made here that the political processes which are protected by the U.S. Constitution for its own citizens are political values that should be conceded to all nations deserving them. The universal extension of our domestic political heritage rules out all unilateral decisions by the United States in the international system since such conduct would involve U.S. citizens in a sort of schizophrenia between its domestic interests and its conduct of foreign policy.

What would have been the consequences for American diplomacy during the '60s of this "assumption that other nations have traditions, interests, values, rights, and obligations of their own"? How would such an assumption have influenced U.S. policy-making, for example, in regard to Vietnam? What, in other words, are the implications of the ethics of partnership for assessing American policies in Southeast Asia?

I once asked a young South Vietnamese friend of mine about the justice of U.S. involvement in the war. His answer was immediate and enlightening: "The U.S. was justified in their involvement until they cooperated in the overthrow of Diem." With no hesitation, he pointed to a time, a place and a decision that marked the turning point between moral assistance and immoral interference: the decision to undermine the recognized government of his country. At this point, my friend suggested, South Vietnam ceased being a partner of the U.S. and became merely a pawn. What had been cooperation became domination, the subjugation of indigenous forces and aspirations to a global U.S. strategy of containment or balance of power. With this switch from involvement on the side of the South Vietnamese to subordination of their interests to the larger purposes of global strategy, the U.S. government embarked on a course of events which could no longer be termed just.

How valid is this private judgment of a friend? Does it reveal anything about the actual political dynamics of the situation and point to a real shift in U.S. intentions? Was the decision to undermine Diem's position a moral turning point in the U.S. involvement in Southeast Asia?

It can be argued, I believe, that the downfall of Diem, encouraged at least indirectly by the U.S., was at least the first clear indication that the intentions of Washington were not simply to support South Vietnam in its struggle, but rather to use Vietnam as a battleground to contain Communism or to demonstrate U.S. resolve and power. The argument will be made here that at least from the fall of Diem onwards, the U.S. involvement could not be justified on moral grounds because from this point onward it was clear that there was no genuine partnership or relationship of reciprocal influence between the two governments. By 1963, at the latest, the influence was unilateral. Washington was taking only its own counsel about the outcome of the war. After 1963 the South Vietnamese were denied an effective voice in the determination of policy concerning the war fought in their homeland: they were effectively excluded from the political debate on the future of their country. In terms, then, of the earlier analysis of the U.S. Constitution and its foreign policy implications, one could conclude that the policy of confining the deci-

sion-making to Washington was inconsistent with our
domestic political heritage. While the Constitution
requires that all interested parties to a decision have a
voice in the shaping of that decision, it seems that the
South Vietnamese were effectively excluded from such
participation in decisions which intimately affected
them. According to this analysis, the partnership
among interests, which characterizes the American political tradition, was denied the Vietnamese. By this
exclusion of the Vietnamese, America involved itself in
a contradiction between its domestic political heritage
and its external policies. It was this moral schizophrenia which, as Schlesinger observes, convulsed the American people. By denying the Vietnamese a voice in the
decisions affecting their future, the Americans were involving themselves in a fundamental political inconsis-
tency which was ironically destined to overturn the
American administration in turn.

It is interesting to observe, in this comparison between the ethics of partnership and more traditional
moral systems, that precisely the same analysis might
have been made of the injustice of the Vietnam involvement from the perspective of just war theory. According to the traditional concepts governing the just use of
violence, only those wars are considered just which
meet five criteria: (1) they must be defensive (just
cause); (2) they must be fought for the right reason
(the just cause mentioned above must be the actual
motivation of those mounting a defensive action; specific defensive measures may not be used as a pretext
for accomplishing other military/political goals, such
as acquiring new territory or pursuing a global strategy
of containment); (3) the defense must be proportionate
to the injustice to be corrected; (4) defensive measures

cannot include the direct attack on non-combatants; (5) there must be a reasonable chance that the defensive effort can successfully redress the aggression. Of these five criteria, the one most clearly violated by the United States in South Vietnam concerns the intention of American involvement. It seems quite likely that almost from the beginning, the contest in South Vietnam was seen by Washington as a significant clash between Communist forces and those opposed to the expansion of Communism, and hence as a contest worthy of being sustained. For some period afterwards (perhaps until 1963), the defensive efforts on behalf of the South Vietnamese Government were probably justified in the effort to protect the non-Communist way of life for the South. From the moment, however, when the leaders in the South began to reconsider the viability of resisting the attacks from the North, and initiated discussions about accommodation with the North, U.S. attitudes and those of the Diem government diverged. At this point, it became clear that Diem's interest in the Vietnamese unification contradicted the U.S. global strategy of containment. When Diem planned to discontinue his government's resistance to unification, the U.S. withdrew its support of the government, with the intention of weakening it, and finally acceded to the planned overthrow of Diem. At this point the rupture of the previous partnership between the two governments was due to a divergence of interests (intentions) between Diem and Washington. The discontinuance of defensive efforts, while judged by Diem to be in his nation's interest, was judged by Washington to contravene U.S. interests. At this point the specific aggression in Vietnam was no longer the cause requiring continued U.S. support of the war, and from this point onward U.S. involvement was immoral according to the traditional categories of the just war theory.

Thus it appears that the ethics of partnership and the just war theory come to the same conclusion about the morality of U.S. involvement in Vietnam after 1963. The denial of a voice to the Vietnamese in the decisions on whether to continue the war or to seek accommodation is sufficient to brand U.S. involvement after 1963 as immoral because this denial contradicted the notion of partnership, which includes reciprocal influence between political partners. Similarly, the U.S. resolve to prosecute the war under a substitute government when Diem sought accommodation with the North represented a clear divergence between the intentions of the government which we had originally sought to defend and our own intentions, which included the prosecution of a global strategy of containment. By either standard, then, the war is seen as immoral because after 1963 Vietnam became a pawn in international politics rather than an independent and autonomous actor in the international system.

3. Beyond the Just War

As a concluding essay in the relationship between partnership and politics, it might be illuminating to re-examine the ultimate moral dilemma confronting mankind: modern war. Does the ethics of partnership offer any insight into the perennial problem of the relation between violence and the moral order? It might seem at first, for example, that the adoption of an ethics of partnership might imply the necessity of adhering to a politics of non-violence such as Gandhi's. For it was Gandhi, after all, who originally conceived of politics as a strategy to resolve conflicts of interest non-violently by engaging one's opponent in an encompassing relationship which would transform enemies into partners. Does partnership imply that conflict always be non-violent, as Gandhi contended? Or would it be possible, on the other hand, to adapt Gandhi's philosophy of partnership to more conventional politics, which include the possible recourse to violence, while still invoking his fundamental insight into political reality?

Conversely, is it possible to inquire about the implications of the ideal of partnership for more traditional ethics, such as the just war theory? If partnership may be compatible with the limited use of violence in the international system, is the just war theory an adequate conceptual model for defining limits to the use of violence? Or, on the other hand, would partnership imply a radically different approach to understanding the goals of war and to criticizing military strategy? Does partnership, in short, open a new path to contemporary man in his attempts to control the escalation of violence? Is partnership a helpful paradigm for interpretation and involvement in international politics?

The establishment of a partnership—a relationship of mutual dependence and reciprocal influence—was Gandhi's political program. In South Africa, in the Ahmedabad strike against the mill owners, and in the London confrontation with the King's government, the Mahatma labored to discover and develop common interests with his adversaries in order to draw them into serious negotiation. Within a context of mutual respect, superficial conflicts of interest would, according to this theory, inevitably yield to the realization of more profound common interests. Adversaries would become partners in the joint resolution of political conflict.

This political strategy was devised by Gandhi on the basis of his fundamental insight into the relationship between truth and politics. Since truth is a many-sided reality, in which each person shares, the discovery of political truth, or adequate solutions to political impasses, depends upon the creation of the proper context in which each partner to the conflict could feel free to advance his position without fear of destruction. To confront one another without destroying one another was seen as the most creative approach to politics. Within such a context, confrontation would give way to a joint realization of some acceptable course of action, a new truth. Around the search for this truth, which could emerge in the respectful conflict of adversaries, Gandhi built both his politics and his religious quest. Both a saint and a politician, the Mahatma sought only to assist in the emergence of that truth which can be generated by the sustained conflict among trusting opponents.

Non-violence was not the goal of this political philosophy, but only a technique—indispensable as it was —to uncover the truth which was unknowingly shared by the adversaries. Since each partner to the conflict possessed an element of the final truth, neither could eliminate his opponent by violence, under pain of forfeiting the truth possessed by the other. Violence was rejected by Gandhi because it would inevitably preclude that fusion of opposed perceptions which create political truth (resolution).

Contrary to popular belief, the fundamental conviction of Gandhi was the *power of truth*. For him, non-violence was only a corollary, a means to an end. That end was truth. Shivesh Thakur (*International Philosophical Quarterly*, December 1971) argues for this priority of truth in Gandhi's philosophy on the basis of two of his statements:

It seems to me that I understand the ideal of truth better than that of *Ahimsa* (non-violence) and my experience tells me that, if I let go my hold of truth, I shall never be able to solve the riddle of *Ahimsa*. (*Gandhi Reader*, page 301)

Ahimsa is a means; truth is the end. (*All Men Are Brothers*, page 81)

For Gandhi, political partnership required nonviolent strategies exclusively. Is it possible, however, to retain the imperative of his political philosophy, while adapting it to conventional national participation in the international system? Is the link which Gandhi saw between partnership and non-violence a necessary one, or could a limited reliance on military force be justified within an ethic of partnership?

In response to this question of adapting Gandhi's truth method to conventional politics, it is helpful to recall that the Mahatma himself admitted to being more certain of his understanding of truth than of non-violence. For him, truth was the goal and non-violence a means. Moreover, it appears that his unwavering insistence on the indispensability of non-violent strategy may even have been inconsistent with the fundamental tenet of his philosophy, which was "a single-minded search for the truth, and a corresponding indifference to all other values." Should this indifference to all other values, which is merely a corollary of his notion of a *single-minded* search for the truth, not include an indifference (flexibility) in regard to non-violence itself? Is it not possible that in some circumstances the search for truth might require reliance on violence? Critics of the Gandhian philosophy, such as Hannah Arendt, point out that an insistence on non-violence might have condemned his political effort to frustration and defeat if he had opposed some less benevolent adversary than the British Empire. Against the forces of Hitler or Stalin, for example, it is quite probable that the dispatching of waves of unarmed women would have availed nothing. Indeed, if one is committed, as Gandhi was, to an enduring confrontation with an adversary until the truth of the situation be wrested from both parties, is it not possible that the truth-method would require armed defense in cases where the conflict would otherwise be ended simply by superior military force?

In response to these critical questions, a pacifist might reply that these efforts at accommodating the truth-method to conventional politics ignores the Gandhian assumption that truth is latent in all parties to a conflict. It was on the basis of this assumption that the killing of an opponent was prohibited, for the elimination of an opponent precludes the discovery of truth, which is always a joint revelation of partners as a result of sustained conflict. These objections from defenders of the integrity of the Gandhian vision overlook a fundamental difference between individual combat, in which the continuing conflict of both partners is required for the discovery of truth, and group combat, such as warfare, in which the two nations can sustain their armed confrontation despite the loss of individual combatants on either side. In the light of this difference between individual and group conflicts, it may be possible, then, to adapt the Gandhian method to conventional politics, which allows the resolution of political disputes to occur through military engagements and which denies that the deaths of individual soldiers preclude the emergence of genuine political solutions to conflict.

Partnership, then, may not require non-violence as an indispensable strategy. On the contrary, partnership among nations may permit, or even require, armed intervention in the course of sustaining serious confrontation on issues of fundamental importance. It may be, then, that Gandhi's insight into the potential reconciliation of adversaries through sustained confrontation can be adapted to conventional politics. Such an adaptation of the Gandhian vision will require the complementary insights of alternative theories of conflict which are more attuned to the realities of international politics.

A conspicuous resource for the understanding of

warfare within the context of politics is the just war theory. (For an outline of the theory, *cf.* the previous section on "National Interest and National Integrity.") Although this ancient tradition itself is in need of profound reassessment in the light of twentieth century developments in technology and politics, several elements of the tradition provide a useful complement to the Gandhian perspectives on power. Primary among the contributions of the just war theory to contemporary political thought are: its acceptance of the limited use of violence as a moral option in response to aggression or injustice; and its clarification of the moral priority of *political goals* over *military strategies* in the event of such a necessary use of force.

Moralists in the just war tradition have for fifteen centuries argued for a middle position between pacifism and unlimited reliance on military force. Christian moralists, in particular, after studying the Scriptures for some definitive solution to the agonizing question of relating morality and warfare, have reluctantly concluded that nothing in the Bible settles the question. Searching the writings of philosophers, poets and theologians over the centuries, they have concluded that we have no certainty that all use of violence against one's fellow human beings is necessarily immoral. The reason for this agnosticism about the moral legitimacy of the use of violence is the realization that the usual attempt to base a theory of non-violence on the absolute inviolability of life involves a contradiction. Advocates of the right of violent self-defense point out that the claim of the inviolability of human life, if made absolutely, obliges the one under attack to defend his own life to the extent of his physical ability. Otherwise, he is failing by omission. If, however, inviolability is not an absolute obligation, neither does it oblige him to spare his attacker's life. It is, then, impossible to conclude that pacifism is the only morally acceptable approach to the problem of violence.

On the basis of this conviction that no certain defense of pacifism has ever been proffered, just war theorists have concentrated their attention on setting limits to the use of military violence by underlining the priority of political goals over military strategies. That is, they put to the strategist (and the statesman) the question: What is the political purpose of this strategy? What (political) goals are being pursued by this use of violence? If the purpose of the strategy is legitimate (to defend against aggression or redress an injustice), the strategy itself is subjected to the second question: Does this strategy represent the minimal use of force necessary to achieve that goal? Is there, furthermore, reasonable assurance that such a strategy can effect the desired goal? On these points, namely, certification of the political goal and measurement of the strategy to the stated political purpose, moralists have erected the —admittedly fragile—theory of the just war. In doing so, they have attempted—unsuccessfully in this century at least—to moderate the use of violence in the achievement of political purposes.

John Courtney Murray, S.J., one of the most knowledgeable, realistic and articulate modern spokesman for the tradition, admitted in a little noticed footnote (*Morality and Modern War*, Council on Religion and International Affairs, page 23, footnote 8) the meager results of this sophisticated theorizing about the justice of war:

I use the subjunctive because I do not know how many

wars in history would stand up under judgment by the traditional norms, or what difference it made at the time whether they did or not.

With this somber assessment, Murray anticipated the melancholy reflection on the history of violence uttered by Hannah Arendt, another defender of the moral legitimacy of violence:

The danger of violence . . . will always be that the means will overwhelm the end . . . the practice of violence changes the world, but the most probable change is to a more violent world. (*Crises of the Republic*, page 177)

Murray came to his conclusion about the ineffectiveness of the just war tradition just fifty years and two world wars after Ernst Troeltsch concluded his massive study (*The Social Teaching of the Christian Churches*) with the opinion that the pacifist/just war debates and similar disputes between sectarian (such as pacifist) and ecclesial (such as just war oriented) approaches to ethics were of no avail. "New thoughts will have to be thought," Troeltsch concluded, if Christians are to come to terms with political ethics.

What is the reason for the ineffectuality of the ancient tradition which attempts to limit war? What "new thoughts" are needed? The remainder of this essay will suggest that even as Troeltsch was writing these words in Germany in 1908, Gandhi was engaged in thinking such new thoughts and in acting upon them. In the Gandhian approach to politics, modified by the admissibility of a limited use of violence, there may lie a philosophy of power on which to build a more viable political ethic. By combining some of the insights of Gandhi and some elements of the just war theory, it may yet be possible to formulate a more satisfactory theory of politics.

The comparison of Gandhi's truth method with the just war theory highlights the fundamental weakness of the scholastic tradition, namely, the absence of any comprehensive philosophy of power to support its analysis of warfare. Through integration of the political realism of the just war tradition (which recognizes and validates the perpetual reliance on military force in the international system) with the Gandhian philosophy of power, it may be possible to articulate a political ethic which may be more effective in assisting statesmen to limit the use of violence in the pursuit of political goals.

Indeed, the elements for such an integration of apparently unrelated political theories seems already to have been suggested by one of America's leading elder statesmen, George Kennan. In various writings which contain his reflections on the lessons of twentieth-century diplomatic and military history, Kennan has articulated a realistic vision of political partnership between adversaries which may provide a key to the reformulation of political ethics in our time.

A clue to Kennan's reformulation of political philosophy is contained in this somber assessment of the feasibility of limited war:

A considerable importance must also be assigned to the seeming inability of the democratic state to cultivate and to hold in mind anything like a realistic image of a wartime adversary. The Nazi movement was in many ways a terrible thing: one of the most fearful manifestations modern history has to show of the delusions to which men are prone and the evil of which they are capable when they cut loose from all inhibitions of method and sell their souls to the pursuit of a total end.

But this movement was not purely an act of God. It was not an evil miracle. It was a human tragedy, and one of which a great many German people were sufferers no less than others. No one would plead that the allies should have blinded themselves to the danger of Hitler's ambition or even to those deficiencies in the German experience and the German character which had made possible his rule. But had the statesmen of the West been able to look at Germany more thoughtfully and more dispassionately, to liberate themselves from the prejudices of World War I, to distinguish ruler from ruled, to search for the true origins of what had occurred, to recognize the measure of responsibility the Western democracies themselves had for the rise of Nazism in the first place, and to remember that it was on the strength and hope of the German people, along with all others, that any tolerable post-war future for Europe would have to be built—had they been able to comprehend all this it would have helped them to understand the relationship of Russia to Germany in the War, to achieve a better balance in their dealings with both of these troublesome and problematic forces and thus, perhaps, to avoid or mitigate some of the most grievous of the War's political consequences. (*Russia and the West Under Lenin and Stalin*, pages 368-369)

Kennan rejects the tendency of nations to sever all human ties with their adversaries, and admonishes: "No other people, as a whole, is entirely our enemy. No people at all—not even ourselves—is entirely our friend." This insistence on the continuing partnership of nations even during hostilities may be the beginning of political wisdom. This perception arose in Kennan's mind as he sought to understand why the allies insisted on the unconditional surrender of Germany and Japan and subsequently, with equal vigor, rebuilt these former enemies into two of its most prosperous post-war allies and most formidable economic competitors. Urging more foresight in diplomacy, Kennan argues that nations must learn to regard one another as permanent partners in the international system who cannot, unlike individual human beings, divorce themselves from one another. The plurality of nations is perpetual and every discrete decision about modes of interaction must be framed within this chronological continuum of mutual dependence and reciprocal influence among nations.

The picture, then, which I hope I have presented is that of an international life in which not only is there nothing final in point of time, nothing not vulnerable to the law of change, but also nothing absolute in itself: a life in which there is no friendship without some element of antagonism; no enmity without some rudimentary community of interest; no benevolent intervention which is not also in part an injury; no active recalcitrance, no seeming evil, from which—as Shakespeare put it—the "soul of goodness" may not be distilled. (*Russia and the West Under Lenin and Stalin*, page 398)

Principal among the policy recommendations which emerge from Kennan's reflections on the first half of the twentieth century was the rejection of the dangerous illusion of total victory in total war. Examining this relatively modern concept and rejecting it as a political or military goal, Kennan urged (in his *Memoirs: 1900-1950*) the return to the civilized concept of "limited war":

This meant, it seemed to me, a need for return to much earlier concepts. The doctrine of total war has been a doctrine of the nineteenth and twentieth centuries. We would now have to revert to the concepts of limited warfare prevalent in the eighteenth century. The aims of warfare, accordingly, would have to become limited. If weapons were to be used at all, they would have to be

employed to temper the ambitions of an adversary, or
to make good limited objectives against his will—not to
destroy his power, or his government, or to disarm him
entirely . . . Man would have to recognize, in short,
that the devices of military coercion could have, in the
future, only relative—never an absolute—value in the
pursuit of political objectives. (*Memoirs*, page 310)

In this conclusion Kennan agreed with the post-war
reflections of John Murray, who consistently recalled
the moral argument to the central problem by insisting:
"The problem is limited war." (*Morality and Modern
War*, page 18) Kennan and Murray likewise agreed that
World War II policies of unconditional surrender and
obliteration and atom-bombing were the most egregious
Allied errors flowing from this illusory political philosophy of total victory.

    Where Kennan, the statesman, and Murray, the
moralist, differ is in the political philosophy within
which they recommend these policy conclusions. For
Murray, the unacceptability of the policy of unconditional surrender and atomic bombing stems from the
traditional just war criteria which subordinate military
strategies to reasonable political goals. Murray's limits
on strategy derived from the defensive nature of warfare. Kennan, however, locates his policy recommendations within a political vision which is larger and
more persuasive than the moral argument advanced by
Murray. Kennan bases his conclusions on a view of
power, which he understands to be the ongoing interaction of complex societies. Each of these competing societies, in turn, is composed of various cultural, political and economic interests which are in competition
among themselves. Various segments of such societies
will urge initiatives unwelcome to other segments of the

society, just as they will respond diversely to initiatives from abroad. Moreover, such societies never become fully identified with the leadership at any given time. Finally, each society expects, and can be expected, to survive any catastrophe in international relations, barring only nuclear holocaust. To recover from a major military disaster, the society will require a functioning economy, which will be exorbitantly expensive to rebuild after indiscriminate military attack. Kennan distinguishes (as Murray did in another context) between societies and their governments. While governments may embark on suicidal policies which may result in national disaster and self-destruction for the leadership, the society itself has a virtual promise of immortality. Consequently, Kennan urges that diplomacy and strategy be designed to check the unreasonable aspirations of the leadership of competing societies without entertaining the illusion that such societies can be eliminated or permanently subjugated. For this reason, he cautions against policies that would threaten the economic organization of competing societies. More positively, he recommends that such societies (in contrast to their leadership) be recognized for what they are, namely, permanent partners in the international system.

The just war tradition, on the other hand, which was elaborated in an ancient culture whose dissimilarity to the twentieth century can hardly be grasped, seems to offer a moral formula without any supporting political vision, or comprehensive philosophy of power. It seems, in other words, to segregate the period of interstate conflict from the chronological continuum within which war forms a tragic moment. Moreover, this tradition seems unduly to isolate the study of military power from considerations of the economic and political forms of organization. Natural law theories, then, may be faulted for maintaining a static view of social relationships and thereby disregarding the possibility of creative interaction among the antagonists in an international conflict. Just war theory could thus be profitably complemented by a more fluid or dynamic interpretation of social reality, such as Gandhi's proposal of the positive value of creative conflict. Since just war thinkers often tacitly assume that national adversaries cannot become partners, they seem to interpret the interaction among nations with an almost physical analogy of colliding bodies. Gandhi's insights (elaborated in historical terms by Kennan) might help to correct the tendency to overlook the specifically social characteristics of human conflict. Political power may be characteristically different from physical power. The implications of this difference were perhaps better understood by Gandhi (and Kennan) than by Grotius (and Murray). Even in war, societies are locked in an indissoluble partnership, which will endure after the cessation of hostilities and the replacement of leaders. When statesmen come to share the wisdom which George Kennan acquired during the tragic events of this century, we may yet recapture and refashion the ancient tradition of civilized warfare.

In assessing the possible contribution of an ethics of partnership to the tradition of civilized warfare, it is important to observe that the newer ethic may transform the just war tradition by adding to it a new restriction on the use of violence. In addition to the traditional condemnation of direct attacks on non-combatants, it may be necessary to condemn all military activities designed to attack directly the non-military economic centers of enemy nations. The reason for adding this prohibition to the existing limits on the use of violence is the realization that a defeated society, which will continue to exist after the cessation of hostilities, has a right to the means of survival, namely, to a functioning economy. After the surrender of Germany and Japan, the United States belatedly realized that only the victorious powers, and specifically, the United States, itself, had the resources to rebuild the economies of its former enemies. The fruit of this tardy realization was the Marshall Plan. Kennan suggests that this triumph of American diplomacy and wealth would have been less burdensome if America had been able during wartime to maintain a more realistic view of its enemies and a long-range view of the functioning of the international system. He seems to recommend, in other words, that in somewhat the same way that Munich dominated the diplomacy of the sixties, so the memory of the Marshall Plan should inspire our diplomacy and strategy of the future, so that we will never forget during hostilities that today's enemies are destined to be tomorrow's allies.

Conclusion

The argument of this book, that contemporary efforts to understand the dynamics of moral life tend to place greater emphasis on the role of social process in moral decision-making than on cognitive principles, will remain the subject of debate for decades to come. In support of the contention that such a profound shift in moral paradigms represents a constructive change, three current issues in political ethics have been analyzed in the present essay. By studying Watergate, U.S. involvement in international diplomacy (especially in Vietnam), and the perennial problem of limited war (with specific application to World War II), we hoped to discover that each of these issues could be illuminated by the criterion of partnership: Did the parties to the dispute seek to maintain with one another a relationship of mutual dependence and reciprocal influence? Would the outcome of these historical incidents have been different if partnership had been an influential consideration for the decision-makers? What light, in short, does the ideal of partnership throw on politics?

The conclusion in each case was that the principal actors, inspired by the ideal of partnership, might have chosen a different course of action, which might have been less damaging to the common weal. Neither the Democratic National Headquarters nor Dr. Fielding's office would have been burglarized because the potential opposition of McGovern and Ellsberg would not have been viewed as a threat to Republican power but as a source of creative conflict; the U.S. might have withdrawn its military support in 1963 when Diem had decided to accept reunification of Vietnam; offers of conditional surrender might have been made to Germany and Japan, shortening the war and precluding the eventual decision to use the atomic bomb.

The attempt to articulate a moral theory, however, is not an effort to rewrite history by hindsight. Even though a moralist may believe that ideas have historical consequences, he is more concerned fundamentally with the correctness of the idea than with the prediction of consequences. Happy consequences, he argues, are at least partially a product of sound ideas. Why does this moralist, then, feel that partnership is a sound moral ideal? What advantage does he see in the current shift of attention from an ethics of principles to one based on partnership?

It was, perhaps, Gandhi who articulated the major reason for a shift away from a moral system based on rational or religious principles to one which seeks solution to moral dilemmas through social conflict. For Gandhi perceived that the quest for moral behavior is but an aspect of the search for *TRUTH*. Morally correct behavior flows almost ineluctably from the clear perception of the truth while immoral behavior is frequently the consequence of a distorted view of the truth. The moral problem, that is, is not so much a failure to do what one knows to be correct as the inability to determine the correct course of action. To overcome the prevalence of ignorance about social conduct, Gandhi counseled a commitment to sustain social conflict, which he felt would reveal the truth of the situation. By resolving to urge one's own position while attentively listening to the opposition, a person has entered into the moral realm. Once a moral agent has made this commitment to speak and to listen, he can rest content that the course of action jointly arrived at will be the best decision that was humanly possible in the situation. The commitment to influence, and to be influenced by, one's opponent is the fundamental moral principle. Implied in the principle, of course, is a commitment to truthfulness, for honest communication of complementary perspectives is the indispensable means of arriving at the truth. Since no individual or interest has a total comprehension of the truth, it is only by sustained conflict between holders of partial truths that the correct course of action can be discerned.

For citizens of some nations, such as the United States, this moral commitment coincides with political allegiance, for constitutional republics are founded on an identical vision: that genuine and lasting power is a function of truth, which can be arrived at only by the open conflict of opposing viewpoints. Pluralism is the safeguard of political power. Americans, then, need not look for some abstruse principle to determine their course of action in domestic political affairs. They need only participate in the political institutions they have inherited. On questions of the domestic common good, legality and morality coincide in such nations.

When they turn to the area of foreign policy, however, citizens of western liberal democracies are liable to ignore the moral question entirely (on the assumption that the absence of an international legal code precludes the possibility of morality in international affairs) or to work for the resolution of international conflict exclusively through the elaboration of legal codes and the institution of international organizations. Here the moralist must point to the fundamental difference between domestic and international politics and resist the efforts to equate legality and morality in international affairs. In place of this identification of law and morality, he will urge that the *spirit* of democratic laws be applied to foreign policy. That is, he will urge that the solutions to international conflicts of interest be sought in a commitment by nations to influence, and to be influenced by, their opposition. While insisting that their voice be heard on disputed questions, statesmen will also resolutely listen to opposing voices and consider the interests being articulated by these voices. Mutual dependence and reciprocal influence will be the freely chosen criterion for conducting foreign affairs, as it is the constitutional pattern for domestic politics. Diplomacy will be consciously fashioned as the art of achieving consensus among allies on broad common purposes. Diplomacy itself will be recognized as a social process which can be conducted so as to uncover the perceptions which have been generated by other cultural traditions. Unlike domestic politics, a diplomacy based on the reciprocity of influence is not mandated by legal codes, and hence requires a more vital commitment to partnership than does domestic constitutionalism. Such a commitment will be efficacious only if it arises from a deep conviction that all cultural traditions possess resources of insight which can illuminate present predicaments.

Even when international conflict has erupted into armed hostilities, statesmen will not settle for being merely strategists, determined to prevail militarily at any cost, but will insist on the subordination of military strategy to political concerns. Adhering to this hierarchy of political purpose over strategy, statesmen will employ military force as a form of communication with their counterparts, and with the nations they represent, without ever entertaining the notion of annihilating these hostile nations or permanently destroying their economic fabric. Even during the hostilities, statesmen will strive to regard their opponents as permanent partners in the international system and will not sacrifice international stability in the future to present prospects of speedy victory. Strategy will always remain an instrument of diplomacy, the art of achieving coordination among nations fated to remain partners in the international system.

Politics, in other words, even the extreme politics of war, should be conducted in the spirit of partnership, of mutual dependence and reciprocal influence. It was Gandhi who saw that the necessity of political partnerships stems from the nature of truth, which is poliarchical. Political partners must strive for reciprocal influence because they depend on one another's perspectives in the search for truth. Truth, finally, defines the limits of politics.